MEMOIRS OF A DEPUTY CORONER:
The Case of Marilyn Monroe

Lionel Grandison Jr.
Samir Muqaddin

Memoirs of a Deputy Coroner:
The Case of Marilyn Monroe

ISBN: 978-0-9859619-1-6

Printed in the United States of America

Table of Contents

ACKNOWLEDGEMENTS

To thank those who have both contributed to this story and in some ways to the completion of this book would take many pages and we would still unintentionally neglect to name someone. But we would not feel this book is complete without furnishing a short list:

We are especially grateful to our loving soul mates, Chanelle and Yvonne. It has been their undying support, encouragement, strength, comfort and warmth that has sustained us all along.

To the third member of our team, Lionel Grandison II, we apologize for the tirades and arguments we had to put you through while writing this book. Thankfully, we can now go back to normal.

We are especially grateful to our editor, Amber Grandison who rushed home after graduation from University of California at Irvine to polish and push the manuscript toward publication.

Joining in to take up some of the slack is Lance Grandison, Crystal Jackson, Alithra "Tipy" Louda, Geoff Gil, Cory Crismon, and Tony James Jr., whose efforts have all been greatly appreciated.

Also included on the list are Veda James, Ora Hutchinson, Minnie Lee Williams, Romie "Bobby" James and Frank & Lolita "Auntie" McCrimmon.

Last, but not least, we humbly dedicate this book to Robert & Debra Slatzer, Jack Clemmons, Jeanne Carmen, Imam Ali Rasheed, and all the people who have put their lives and reputations on the line during the quest to discover Marilyn's true cause of death.

FROM THE AUTHOR

Most people grow up with an image of their parents that remains with them for a large part of their lives. It is imprinted upon us from the time of birth and quickly evolves into our own reality. Then suddenly, one day after our parents have gotten older and usually we have too, like magic, you begin to see them differently. Sometimes it may be good and sometimes not so much, but it's always illuminating.

Two years ago, I decided to write a book about my father's experiences with the case of Marilyn Monroe. For those of you who don't know, my dad was the Los Angeles County Deputy Coroner, who signed her death certificate. During his investigation, he witnessed a cover-up of epic proportions and was forced to pay a huge price because of his discovery of Marilyn's secret diary.

The decision to write this book was due to my father's completion of his memoirs, which included every detail he had ever written or investigated regarding Marilyn Monroe's case during the past 50 years. When he brought me his papers, I was stunned by the story he had told.

Although I'd grown up hearing about his ordeal and experienced some of its aftermath, many years had passed since the subject of Marilyn's death resurfaced. By then, I had been married for 20 years had 2 children of my own.

My daughter was already a junior in college with medical school in her sights, and my son was working with me in our family business. Neither of them knew the story of Marilyn Monroe, much less that their Grandfather had been involved. After reading my father's memoirs, I knew it was time for that to change.

It is difficult to explain the impact his memoirs had on me. When I began to read his innermost thoughts about Marilyn's case and how it impacted his life, almost inexplicably something changed. I began to see my father differently and understand the man he truly was. His story was riveting, and when my reading was complete, I knew this information had to be published for the world to see.

Before beginning to write this book, I shared the memoirs with some friends of mine in the entertainment industry. They were just as floored as I was. One of them later called and said he had a major Hollywood producer who wanted to do a film about my father's life. This producer, whose film credits included, "The Butterfly Effect" starring Ashton Kutcher and "Lucky Number Slevin" starring Bruce Willis, invited my dad and I to his home in the Hollywood Hills, offering to purchase the story rights.

At the time, he was in the middle of producing "The

Rum Diaries" starring Johnny Depp, but we signed the deal and later did a huge story with Variety Magazine about our upcoming movie. Ultimately, the producer encountered some difficulties and the deal was cancelled. Meanwhile, I began writing this book, spending long hours going through my dad's memoirs and talking to him about the case of Marilyn Monroe.

His recollections and accounts about the people involved were mesmerizing. He provided in-depth details about the days following Marilyn's death and what transpired at the coroner's office. He talked about his personal relationships in 1962, with Los Angeles County Chief Medical Examiner, Theodore Curphey and also the man who performed the autopsy, Dr. Thomas Noguchi. My father personally knew nearly everybody involved with the official case.

He talked about being only 22 years old when he walked into the office that Sunday morning and discovered her case was assigned to him. His memoirs thoroughly described the drama that followed including finding her diary in the property recovered in from her house. Although I'd seen his diary notes before, subsequent years of his investigation made the information even more pertinent.

Interestingly enough, during my early twenties, I had encouraged my father to begin writing his memoirs. In fact, with the help of my younger sister and brother, I began organizing all of his research papers, including the diary notes. We transferred nearly everything to floppy discs and gave it all to him for whenever he decided to begin writing. That was the last time we talked about his memoirs.

While writing the book, I was also reminded of all the drama our family endured during the historic 1982 District Attorney's Inquiry into Marilyn Monroe's death. Most people have never experienced what it feels like when the news media decides you're the hot story. During the 82' Inquiry, our neighborhood was under siege with news trucks and reporters hounding our house like you'd never believe.

They persistently asked questions, harassing us and making life miserable for everyone.

To be honest, I really didn't understand what was happening during that time. But after reading through the memoirs, my father explained details about that inquiry I never knew. He wrote about how lead investigator, Assistant District Attorney Ronald Carroll, tried to intimidate him and what was said during his interview with my father. He painted a picture most people never understood about the investigation, revealing how the District Attorney's office really wasn't trying to discover the truth.

Ronald Carroll died not long after my father completed his memoir. The Los Angeles Times wrote a very interesting obituary story about him, describing the 82' inquiry and how my father's statements were the primary reason for launching the District Attorney's investigation. Although Carroll would eventually chose to agree with the evidence of Marilyn committing suicide, my father never waivered from his quest to discover truth.

Having investigated Marilyn's case for half a century, my father has identified the facts surrounding her death like never before. The information is mind-boggling and connects the dots where other journalists have failed. I really believe readers will discover a Marilyn Monroe they never knew and gain a true understanding of what likely happened to her.

What is more important, now that our book is complete, is my understanding of what this amazing man went through. His struggles to reveal the truth about Marilyn Monroe's death have led me to believe my father, Lionel Grandison, is an American hero. My only hope now is that by reading the book, more people will understand how he fought for Marilyn and the high price he paid.

PREFACE

Throughout literary history the old cliché "truth is stranger than fiction" is one of the most infamous ones. However, never in my wildest dreams did I think this oft-used term could describe a fifty-year span of my life. The true story I am about to present is compelling as any detective novel or Sci-Fi thriller. It covers my unlikely experience with the life and death of a public figure who was perhaps the most fascinating movie star ever.

The legend of Marilyn Monroe may well be Hollywood's biggest story. Her friends adored her, fans idolized her, and powerful men were drawn to her. However, to quote another cliché, "things were not as they seemed." Marilyn had secrets. She wrote about them in a little red book that I happened to read. It is my belief that she intended to reveal these secrets, but her lips were forever silenced one summer night in 1962 at her Los Angeles home.

As fate would have it, I crossed paths with Marilyn Monroe and her diary the day following her death. This would begin a chain of events that forever changed my life. What I read in that book and my first hand involvement in the investigation of her death has led to me to tell this personal story over 5 decades in the making.

While investigating the circumstances surrounding her death, both as a public official and private citizen, my life became the target of those trying to cover up the truth. For many years I have been silent, but now I'm willing to tell my story, one final time.

There has been a conspiracy to cover up the circumstances surrounding Marilyn's death for a half-century. Certain, seemingly earnest, law enforcement investigators, publicists, and politicians have informed the public that the presented evidence indicated suicide. With conviction, they passed on information given by so-called medical experts, including the Los Angeles County Coroner, without ever presenting all the evidence. This has left the task of revealing the ugly facts of the case to journalists and people like me.

I began organizing my memoirs and gathering my notes on Marilyn's diary in 1978. This came after meeting a journalist who encouraged me to come forward with my first hand knowledge of what happened at the Coroner's Office. He held the belief that Marilyn was murdered and that government officials were involved. Together we would mount a challenging effort to re-open the case.

This book is my attempt to set the record straight on Coroner's Case# 81128. As a Deputy Coroner's Aide for the County of Los Angeles, I was assigned to assist the Medical Examiner in gathering all the necessary evidence to investigate Marilyn's cause of death. The question of how she died was never answered and reluctantly, I signed her Death Certificate.

No conclusion was ever reached as to what pills she took or who prescribed them. I have taken that evidence, along with everything I know about this case, and combined it with updated research such as FBI and CIA disclosures to shed new light on this 50-year old mystery.

In 2010, a new document was released under the Freedom of Information Act, verifying that the Central Intelligence Agency was bugging Marilyn's house the night she died. Since nearly 50 years had passed before the information was released, a valid explanation of the United States Government's involvement in Marilyn Monroe's death could still be a long time coming.

In Marilyn's writings and in my investigation, I discovered complications in her life that had scared off the Los Angeles Police Department and County Officials, and were serious enough to get her killed.

The memoir I have written is a culmination of my life experiences and case research supported by eyewitness accounts, published works, and government documents. It is my personal story about the case of Marilyn Monroe. The only thing that remains is for you to sit down and digest it.

CHAPTER 1:
Introduction to a Conspiracy

I picked up the Los Angeles Times in 2010 and read that Ronald Carroll, a retired Los Angeles County District Attorney had died. He was involved in a number of high profile cases and headed a 1982 review of actress Marilyn Monroe's death in 1962. I further discovered from the article that during a 33-year career in the District Attorney's office, beginning in 1966, Carroll also served as Chief Prosecutor in the highly publicized trial that resulted from a four-hour gun battle between the Black Panthers and police in 1969.

It was very interesting that the Los Angeles Times chose these two cases to highlight his career, as both required a vigorous concealment of facts to keep the truth from the public. However, for me it was something much more personal. You see, these two cases mirrored a 50-year reflection of my life and involvement with perhaps the largest cover-up of the 20th century.

The article went on to say that in 1982 Carroll was assigned to conduct a "threshold inquiry" to determine whether a full-scale homicide investigation of Monroe's death was justified. They had been urged to investigate charges by a former Deputy Coroner, who said that a diary purportedly kept by Monroe had disappeared from the Coroner's Office. He also alleged, "the diary contained the names of key government officials and conversations relating to sensitive government matters."

The Los Angeles Times article was referring to the last official inquiry into the strange death of Marilyn Monroe. This Inquiry was the result of my statements to Los Angeles County Officials that the true cause of death had not been properly determined.

Assistant District Attorney Carroll interviewed me during his inquiry and I told him the Coroner's investigation into the cause of death had been a farce and the diary described many activities she was involved in. Despite the testimony, Carroll said he did not find any credible evidence that the Coroners Office was ever in possession of a diary. He completely disregarded the fact that three other witnesses testified to seeing the book and other key evidence suggesting its presence. The Times reported, and Carroll concluded, that a murder of Monroe, fitting known facts of her death, would have required a massive conspiracy.

When the Los Angeles County District Attorney ignored the evidence and chose not to investigate Marilyn's death, it missed a very special opportunity; to collect the sworn testimony of all the key witnesses who were still alive. As it turned out, this Inquiry, along with the other investigative probes, was all part of the so-called massive conspiracy to cover up evidence in the Marilyn Monroe case.

Twenty years earlier, the Los Angeles County Coroner and the Los Angeles Police Department had also covered-up evidence during their investigation. For them, the case was simply too hot to handle. From what we know now, they would've had to been prepared to subpoena evidence from the Federal Bureau of Investigation and Central Intelligence Agency, including sensitive notes and memos. They also would have needed to question a prestigious member of one of America's most powerful and influential families. Judging by their actions, they neither had the fortitude or determination for that.

All the information that could have been obtained from those sources would have gone a long way toward clearing up the mystery surrounding Marilyn's death. In my mind, those investigations were part of a complex conspiracy that has baffled the public ever since that time.

Today the vision of what really happened to Marilyn Monroe can only be reflections of the startling truth portrayed in a realistic elaboration of the known facts. It is hardly surprising when such information is disseminated to the general public, it is apt to cause certain pessimism. The immediate reaction is that if any social or political problems existed, they would have been revealed by those best equipped for solving it.

To those who don't remember her, Marilyn Monroe was Hollywood. Fifty years after her death, she remained one of the most beloved and controversial women in history. To men, she was the ultimate sex symbol, to women, she was either adored or despised, and to Hollywood she was always good for a front-page cover story in gossip magazines or major newspapers. Since her death, her estate has made twenty times more money than she ever made in her life.

Only one of her films was actually a box office smash, but the camera always found her nonetheless. Her walk, smile, and appearance were her biggest assets but behind the bright lights, this brave woman had been lured into a cloak and dagger lifestyle.

The core of this story is a journal or diary allegedly written by Monroe, which in her own words she wrote accounts of the last ten or so years of her life. I got a glimpse of her complicated world after reading the diary at the Los Angeles County Coroner's Office the day after she died, when a purse containing a little red book was put on my desk labeled "Marilyn Monroe property".

In that book, Marilyn kept a detailed description of events in her life, the centerpiece in this saga. The book disappeared from Los Angeles County Coroner's Office days after it was brought in from her house and has never been recovered.

It seems amazing that we remember her as an emotionally disturbed suicidal woman who was destined for this ending. Nothing in that diary gave me such an impression. If she was depressed or had entertained the idea of suicide, it was only out of fear of what she was involved in. This conspiracy to classify her as suicidal seems to be a fragment of an overall plot by those obscuring the truth. Maybe she wrote her suicidal intentions in another book, and there have been two or 3 other accounts of journals mentioned over the years, but I only saw this one.

The essence of her notes developed an intricate series of events that made me wonder if she was murdered simply because she knew too much. I witnessed a cover-up of the facts that not only affected the Coroner's investigation but other law enforcement agencies. Questions about her involvement with the Intelligence Community and what part the Kennedy White House played in this massive conspiracy to cover-up the truth still go unanswered. I feel strongly that a Coroner's inquest would have brought forth the necessary evidence to determine the true cause of death, thereby forcing the police to investigate more thoroughly.

In my investigation, information given to the authorities by Marilyn's doctors, Ralph Greenson and Hyman Engelberg, was never supported by the facts. Dr. Engelberg said that in his professional opinion it had been the pills he prescribed that caused Marilyn's death. Dr. Greenson, her psychiatrist, said Marilyn had been depressed and was suicidal.

The sworn depositions led to the easily accepted conclusion of her suicidal death, but these doctors were both guilty of misleading authorities. Evidence of a more sinister set of circumstances has emerged.

The Los Angeles Police Department took the approach of using the doctor's statements in reaching their final conclusion. The Coroner's ruling of Probable Suicide was enough for them to discount whatever other evidence they were uncomfortable with.

While at the Coroner's Office, I had conversations with Dr. Theodore Curphey, Coroner of Los Angeles County, Dr. Thomas Noguchi, who did the autopsy, Dr. Ralph Abernathy, who did the toxicology test, the Suicide Investigation Team, and numerous police officers present at the crime scene. None of them could offer a credible answer as to what killed her.

Although Public officials were hesitant to get involved with the politics of Marilyn's death, it has now become apparent to me that the public has kept this story alive. For 50 years they have questioned their picture of legal institutions as pursuers of justice, and the reality of deceitful collusion involving high officials. Such collusion totally discounts the value of life, particularly in the death of a universally loved personality like Marilyn Monroe.

In the context of public perception, even when the official investigation proclaimed suicide, it hardly changed the attitude of the American people. Their thirst for the truth has endured, inspiring numerous publishers, researchers, producers, journalists, and investigators to go on looking for clues as to what really happened.

Now who am I? Who is this man that has spent almost all of his adult life answering questions and investigating the death of a Hollywood icon? In 1962, I was a happily married 22-year old man with 3 children and employed by the County of Los Angeles as a Deputy Coroner's Aide. I had transferred to the Coroner's office as a supervising clerk in 1960, promoted in 1961 to this higher position. My job at the Los Angeles County Coroner's Office was to investigate deaths in the County and ensure all the laws of the State of California were upheld.

I had taken advantage of the new state of hiring put in place following World War II. Race could no longer be an issue in civil service hiring. Minorities could pass an exam and be put on a list that guaranteed consideration for employment within the County, City, State and Federal Governments. Jobs like Deputy Coroner were now available if you were qualified, and if you were number one on the test exam, it was hard to justify being turning down for the position.

Coming out of the bus boycotts, sit-ins, and freedom rides of the 1950's, it was important to me for all Americans to receive equal protection under the law. Working for the Los Angeles County Coroner's office was a privilege taken very seriously. I understood the significance of that position and embraced that responsibility. For me, in this new era, things were not going to be business as usual in County Government when it came to the ordinances governing the rights of citizens.

So when the Coroner, Police, District Attorney or any other agency with a perceived sense of power came to me with something that was outside the legal parameters, I called them out. Never did I go along with something that wasn't ethical and my reputation developed as a straight shooter, who would follow the letter of the law, even when it was not popular.

Recognizing my thorough and fair approach, department supervisors began using me to clear up issues in the minority community. Cases where families were fighting over who was in charge of the burial, or having disagreements with the Coroner's findings were sent to me.

During that time, African American and Latino mortuaries were unfairly being targeted by a discriminating tradition of not designating them as Coroner's representatives. This practice created a different standard of rules and placed these minority owned mortuaries at a competitive disadvantage. Whenever they complained they were sent to me.

In the Investigation Department of the Coroner's Office, there were about six or more deputies assigned to high profile cases needing extensive police investigation. This also required working closely with the Autopsy Surgeons. Other Deputies worked our first-call desk, gathering medical information and police reports for the files. All of us signed death certificates once the cases were closed. In the medical department, there was a pool of stenographers, some laboratory chemists, file clerks, and another 20 or more Deputies who picked up the bodies and gathered evidence from the scene.

The Chief Medical Examiner/Coroner was Dr. Theodore Curphey. He was one of the highest appointed officials in the County of Los Angeles. His duties included:

1.   Responsibility for determining the cause of death of any person who didn't have an attending physician.

2.   Investigating any death with a traumatic injury caused by an accident or at the hands of another.

3.   Investigating all homicides and suicides.

To reach his verdict, the Coroner could call upon the resources of all police departments, the L.A. County District Attorney, Los Angeles City Attorney, and even the State or Federal government agencies in matters of death. The Coroner had the power to convene an inquest and subpoena witnesses to testify; thus his staff had the responsibility of assuring the accuracy of medical facts, police evidence, and proper identification of the deceased. The most important aspect of the initial hours or days was notifying the next of kin for burial, because the County morgue was not a place where relatives wanted their love ones to be.

Most of the cases were normal with identifiable causes of death, submitted by attending physicians, but murders, suicides, accidental deaths and traffic fatalities were more challenging. All police departments in Los Angeles County provided detectives to investigate the facts for the Coroner and scrutinize medical opinions that didn't agree with the circumstances.

With Beverly Hills and Hollywood being part of Los Angeles County, we often dealt with deaths involving the rich and famous. These cases usually involved high-powered attorneys and investigators, who were concerned about estate or insurance issues. So whenever the story began getting a little complicated, usually a spin-doctor was busy at work.

My personal experiences with the Marilyn Monroe case come from the official Coroner's Office investigation, District Attorney, and Grand Jury Inquiries as well as numerous television interviews. They include years of researching government disclosures, journalistic reports, and newspaper accounts of the facts. It adds to what is by now an extensive list of investigations by numerous journalists and researchers, who have examined the suicide question.

Although my observations were not taken seriously at first, recent CIA disclosures have verified many of my accounts. Certain things that Marilyn had addressed in her diary had really transpired. So we can assume most, if not all, of her written passages possessed veracity. With that said, it wasn't until many years later that I began to realize the social significance of the words.

In the mid 1970's, I finally met someone who had actually seen the book and held extensive knowledge of Marilyn's case. The information he shared allowed me to put faces to many names that Marilyn had written about and connected details from her case like never before. This person was journalist Robert Slatzer, one of the foremost authorities on the subject of Marilyn Monroe. Together, we spent many years of investigative research uncovering the facts about Marilyn's death and validating what was in the diary.

Since that time, there have been numerous television interviews and press conferences, along with radio, newspaper and magazine interviews where I have expressed my argument against the suicide claim. My story has even been told to the Los Angeles County Board of Supervisors, who then recommended a grand jury investigation of her death.

Over the years, I have had a chance hear and witness many unsettling accounts of those who reported on what happened. Being the deputy coroner who investigated Marilyn's case, I have been afforded the advantage of observing many of the events that occurred after she died; so my perspective may be more creditable. Above all, what is most compelling about my story is the journal or diary allegedly written by Marilyn Monroe. During my investigation, I was in possession of her official case files and logged her property. Over a two-day period, I read the journal and took notes in order to aid my investigation.

In all of my testimony over the years, I have never gone into detail about what was in the book because it was incriminating, intimidating, and politically sensitive. Although it provided a long list of associates and suspects, the diary never directly stated who killed her. The District Attorney never wanted to talk about the names mentioned in the diary, and though many people claimed to have seen Marilyn's diary, it never became public.

I cannot one hundred percent verify she wrote it, although I did compare it with other handwriting samples in her property. One of my investigative responsibilities at the Coroner's Office was to compare suicide notes with other documents written by the deceased person. Her driver's license signature, some papers in her purse, and some legal documents I was able to obtain had led me to believe the diary was legitimately written by Marilyn.

The diary told an intriguing tale of what she was involved in, who was involved and how she felt about it. As I looked at her passages, I was particularly impressed with how Marilyn kept her thoughts in tact during an ordeal that would have made most of us cringe. If you had the CIA, FBI, Secret Service, Mafia, and the Kennedy family mad enough to kill you, what would you do?

It has taken me a long time to articulate a valid interpretation of what I read. Her observations needed to be researched and taken seriously for what it suggests about twentieth century America. Many other journalists concur with the accounts in Marilyn's diary and have verified her involvement with the intelligence community.

Much has happened to me since reading the diary and being involved in her official case, providing all the real life drama one could ever need. I have been threatened, harassed, embarrassed, charged with a crime, and had my marriage destroyed because of what I learned and my overall connection with the Marilyn Monroe investigation. Despite these difficult situations, I knew my resolve and that my good character would see me through if the truth was known.

CHAPTER 2:
Sign of the Times

First, let me set the stage with my assessment of what was happening in America following World War II. Two movements that were destined to change America forever were starting to take root. During the late 1940s and early 1950s, almost every federal agency had become involved in the anti-Communist and anti Civil Rights crusade. The actions of the federal government helped to forge and legitimize the serious violations of civil liberties that characterized the Senator Joe McCarthy era. It was a cold war period that fueled fears of widespread communism in America.

In this atmosphere the Central Intelligence Agency was created to make a fully functional intelligence office. The CIA was responsible for coordinating the nation's intelligence activities and correlating, evaluating and disseminating intelligence affecting national security. Their methods ranged far beyond international intelligence gathering, and ultimately the organization began domestic operations that would exceed their congressional mandate.

The media was the government's partner, largely because

it amplified messages that came from Washington. After all,

much of the news I heard on the radio or saw in the newspapers simply reported the government's doings.Presidential orders, congressional hearings, and criminal prosecutions all told stories that helped fuel the attacks on the constitutional rights of American citizens.

This was the world Marilyn Monroe found herself in during the early 1950's. Ironically, Marilyn's own writings related the extent of Communist penetration in Hollywood as she wrote about the amount of Communists she had come to know. One of her husbands, writer Arthur Miller, was considered the greatest dramatist of the 20th century and a known Communist sympathizer. The House Un-American Activities Committee would investigate him during its investigation of Communist activity within the film industry.

As the FBI headed into the middle of the decade, a rising challenge based on the age-old problem of racial prejudice, would soon dominate the national stage and require the Bureau's growing involvement. Agency Director, J. Edgar Hoover accused Civil Rights activists, Labor leaders, and Hollywood writers of being communists for challenging the laws of the land.

When political trials, and other traditional legal modes of control failed to counter the growing movements, and even helped to stimulate them, the FBI and police moved outside the law. They resorted to the secret and systematic use of fraud, deceit, and force to sabotage constitutionally protected political activity.

The former General of the Army, Dwight D. Eisenhower was elected President to lead the country through these difficult times. As he left office he said to beware of these agencies and the military complex because the power and money that was being bestowed upon them could corrupt the country.

Meanwhile America's middle class citizens began to mobilize with their own agenda. Organized Labor unions began to provide an economic base for this new class of citizen who wanted to be included in the American dream. The unions were run by a seedy group of people that included Organized Crime figures to help them in their negotiations for wages with the corporate power structure. After years of frustration since the turn of the century, workers didn't care who they partnered with to achieve their goals.

Congressional committees were empowered to fight the labor movement under the banner of resisting communist and socialist domination of the world. The FBI maintained this position while serving legal indictments against Americans Hoover called socialist instigators.

During the decade, Former United States Ambassador Joe Kennedy introduced his two sons, John and Robert, to the political landscape. His sons brought a new image to politics, young, good looking, articulate, Harvard educated, and someone the new middle class could identify with.

John Kennedy served in the House of Representatives (1947-1953) and in the U.S. Senate (1953-1960). He gained national prominence while serving on the Senate Select Committee on Improper Activities in the Labor and Management Field, which held public hearings to investigate corruption in American labor unions.

Robert Kennedy made a name for himself as the chief counsel of the Senate Labor Rackets Committee, which was trying to indict Jimmy Hoffa. In a dramatic scene, Kennedy squared off with the Teamsters union President during the antagonistic argument that marked Kennedy's introduction to mainstream America. Kennedy left the Committee in order to run his brother's successful presidential campaign.

John was already having an affair with Marilyn when he was elected President. During that time, she was actively involved with CIA activities both in America and abroad. Marilyn was young, ambitious, and talented but even these qualities would not last long in this tough environment. For that matter, neither did the Kennedy's. As fate would have it, all three were destined for assassination.

Both John and Robert were sexually and politically involved with Monroe. They took her to meetings where sensitive government matters were being discussed, placing her in an inescapable dangerous environment during the last two years of her.

After reading Marilyn's diary and investigating her case, I found myself also unable to escape. When the wrath of the higher ups came down upon me for my unyielding determination to find the true cause of death, my whole world turned into a nightmare.

I was a young African-American charged with the responsibility of gathering and verifying the circumstances surrounding her death. Although this strange case unfolded right in front of my eyes, I never saw it coming. Little did I know, or could have imagined, how that would impact the rest of my life.

Many have tried to tell the Marilyn story, some good, some bad, some self-serving, some helpful, some Kennedy influenced, and some CIA inspired. The problem was that many readers would perhaps be inclined to see the works as just another conspiracy theory or a typical look into the life of a troubled Hollywood personality.

At this time, I will take my turn explaining what happened to Marilyn, what she wrote in her diary, and why the details of her death were hidden from the public. If it doesn't cause you to think about America's laws, politics, democracy, national security, the superrich, middle class, and overall national character, you will have missed the broader significance of my experiences. I'm going to also relate some of the inexplicable things that happened to me just because I crossed paths with Marilyn Monroe and that bleeping diary.

So in the words of a brilliant writer, I remember it as though it was yesterday.

CHAPTER 3:
One Day at the Office

On Sunday, August 5, 1962, I was working the weekend shift at the Los Angeles County Coroner's Office. It was about a thirty-five minute drive from my house in the San Fernando Valley to downtown Los Angeles. There was little or no traffic on the freeway, so I remember coming into the parking lot in a good mood about ten minutes to eight. The office was in the Hall of Justice, which also housed the Los Angeles County Sheriff and District Attorney.

As I walked in, Deputy Coroner's Aide Albert Stiller told me our supervising Deputy, Phillip Schwartzberg, had assigned me a hot case and it was on my desk. Stiller, who would work the Sunday shift with me, was a 15-year veteran of the Coroner's Office and very knowledgeable about procedure. Phil, our immediate boss, had worked for the County 25 years. He called every, and I do mean every morning at 5:00 AM to give assignments for homicide and other high profile cases.

As I remember, there were about ten or fifteen new cases that night, but figured if Schwartzberg had singled out this particular case, it needed the most attention. Deputy Cronkright had received the first report of the death of Marilyn Monroe from Dr. Ralph Greenson and Dr. Hyman Engelberg sometimes between 4 and 5 AM. Armand Dela Rosa, one of the clerks who handled public inquiries, hung up the phone and said,

"This Marilyn Monroe thing is already crazy. I just came in today to clear some of my cases, and within 30 minutes, at least twenty-five people have called to inquire about her death. You see those lights blinking on the phone? Well, they are all calling about Marilyn. I'm going back home. Good luck to you Lionel and whoever else is working today."

Armand and I were the youngest employees in the office, and had competed for the Deputy Coroner position I had. Most of the employees appreciated the long-term job security in the Coroner's Office and the sense of doing something for society. It had been eight years since the Deputy Coroner job title opened up and all you had to do was what you were told.

Sitting down at my desk that Sunday morning, the paperwork revealed the startling news. The police were reporting the actress died of an apparent drug overdose. Deputy Cronkright had written that 20th Century Fox Studio signed a release of Marilyn's body, saying they could handle the burial. However, removal of her body still required approval by the Coroner's Office.

The Studio and her doctors told our office that they were sure it was a common drug overdose and asked if we could release the body to Westwood Mortuary. As the Deputy in charge, it was my call. Although it was common practice to deputize a Mortuary to act on behalf of the Coroner, the circumstances must completely rule out the need for a complete autopsy with organ examination or the possibility of death at the hands of another.

With high profile cases like these, there generally comes a high degree of scrutiny, so I picked up the phone and called Marilyn's house. Police detectives were still at the scene, and lead investigator Sergeant R.E. Byron took my call. I told him there was additional information needed before we could release her remains, but he told me that her body had already been taken to Westwood mortuary. When I asked who authorized its release, Byron told me to hold for a moment. After returning a few minutes later, he reluctantly stated,

"Mrs. Monroe's remains were authorized for release by Peter Lawford, her friend, and 20th Century Fox, her employer."

Thinking that a little odd, I replied, "Who is the next of kin responsible for her burial?"

Apparently stumped by my question, the officer replied, "There were no known relatives present."

In a death such as this, California State Law prohibited

the release of a body, without next of kin authorization. Thanking the officer, I hung up the phone and immediately called Westwood Mortuary, ordering them to return Marilyn's remains to the house.

Coroner's Deputies were immediately dispatched to bring her downtown to the Hall of Justice for further investigation. The Coroner's representatives were instructed to ask the police for information regarding the doctors who reported the case, any extenuating circumstances, any suicide note, any witness statements, pill bottles, prescriptions, and the names of any relatives that were at the house.

The case had begun rather strangely with LAPD and a reputable mortuary trying to remove her body. Despite thinking this was odd, I never would have envisioned the body and property taking almost 50 years to investigate. But, as I found out later, the Coroner's Office turned out to be part two of the cover up and would take place on my watch. There would be many other cover-ups to follow.

Previous experience with high profile cases had taught me that the scrutiny that comes with these investigations could make or break your future in this office. Months earlier, I was working the graveyard shift and received a call from a California Highway Patrol officer who said comedian, Ernie Kovacs had been killed in an automobile accident.

Kovacs was a Las Vegas headliner, who also had an Emmy nominated network television series in his resume. He died when his car crashed in the hills above Sunset Boulevard in Hollywood.

Pierce Brothers Mortuary was already there with a pre-need authorization from the family to remove the body. A pre-need is a funeral arrangement made by a person before their death. For me, this is always a red flag. It meant that someone had notified a mortuary before they had called the Coroner in an automobile fatality. This would be common in a natural death, but when a police agency responsible for the investigation calls the mortuary first, it is not proper. He went on to say that no one else was involved and no alcohol was detected.

    The Officer ordered me to make note of his conclusions on my report, which led me to determine the case was shaky. I told the officer we would dispatch Coroner's representatives to pick up the remains and to tell the mortuary they could pick up Mr. Kovacs downtown. He vehemently protested my decision, but as a Coroner's representative, I always had authority in accident cases.

The next morning Kovacs' wife, singer Edie Adams and actor Jack Lemmon were awaiting Dr. Curphey when he came into the office. Curphey, who arrived a little earlier than usual, looked at me when he walked in and said,

"Don't go home yet, we need to talk."

After his meeting with the others, Curphey called me in to question my judgment in handling the case, stating when police tell you that everything is alright in a high profile case, it should be taken as fact and their advise followed.

This was my first experience with intimidation while employed as a Los Angeles County Deputy Coroner. Curphey was trying to hinder my investigation of the facts with fear of external pressure from those in powerful places, and this wouldn't be the only time. A few days later the toxicology report showed double the amount of alcohol in the blood allowable under state law. When I presented these results to Dr. Curphey, his response was, "Don't ever question my authority again."

Information also came in from an insurance company investigator on a million dollar double indemnity policy containing a clause stating no payment would be made if Kovacs died from the result of an alcohol related incident. This taught me the lesson that Millions of dollars were involved in these investigations and there is always more than what appears on the surface. I'm sure Mrs. Kovacs and a few others hated me for the rest of their lives.

By the time Marilyn's body got downtown, the office was frantic with phone calls. Newspapers from around the world wanted to know if her death was a suicide as it was being reported. Fox Studios and LAPD were already issuing press releases and holding press conferences describing her death as a suicide. I spent most of the afternoon on the phone, telling people we didn't have any information and the cause of death was pending the autopsy. You should have heard some of the things they said.

Finally Coroner's representative Danbacker, who had

picked up the body from the house, brought the medical information and personal property to my desk. Fox Studios couldn't produce a document with her signature on it that authorized them to handle funeral arraignments. I asked him if the police knew of any next of kin and he told me she apparently had a mother alive in a sanitarium, but no husband, no kids, and apparently no other family members.

Danbacker said there was no suicide note, but noticed that she had died much earlier than reported. A filing cabinet that apparently contained some of her personal papers had been forcibly opened and the housekeeper, Eunice Murray, said no will was found. Marilyn's property consisted of a purse with a wallet, some charge cards, about $30 in cash, and a middle sized book or journal. There was some jewelry, receipts, prescription containers, and a paper flyer announcing a press conference.

Looking through her property, I picked up the book and commenced my search for anything that would reveal an executor or next of kin. It appeared to be a diary about the size of a notebook. I opened the cover and began to read trying to find anything, which would assist my investigation.

The opening page simply stated,

"This is for all the people who ever called me a dumb blond. I may be insecure, but not stupid. I only want to twinkle."

Those beginning words were striking but didn't completely prepare me for the intellectual nature of the book, and as I began scanning through it some very interesting entries appeared on almost every page. I found several phone numbers without names or addresses associated with them. It didn't take me long to realize this was a very special book.

As I continued thumbing through the pages it became impossible to ignore the depth of what was written in this book. It contained names straight out of the headlines of the national newspapers. There were enough hot entries for all the Hollywood gossip magazines to fill their pages. I saw notes making reference to President Kennedy, the FBI, and even people she referred to as "the spy boys." I noticed words such as communist, assassination, Castro, and even Jimmy Hoffa.

On that day, it was difficult to concentrate on the explosiveness of what I was reading. The phone lines were blowing up and things around the office were completely in disarray. Members of the press were all over, clamoring for what was turning out to be the story of the year. I decided to log the contents of her purse and put the property in the safe. My shift was ending soon and it had been a long day. I made some notes for Monday, cleared up my desk and went home.

When I arrived home, the neighborhood was abuzz with the news of Marilyn's death. My wife said all of our friends who knew I worked at the Coroner's Office were calling to get the inside story. Marilyn Monroe was idolized by the general public and from what I had read in her notes some of the private sector too.

I remember sitting on the couch and telling my wife about the diary and what I saw in it. Her reaction was predictable. She said, "Are you serious?" I told her yes and mentioned more of what I read. She just looked at me. At that moment, my son Lance crawled over and she picked him up. I'll never forget the look in her eyes as she held our child. She said,

"That book sounds like trouble. Trouble for you and trouble for us. Those are other people's problems. Do you really want to get involved? The President, Communist, and FBI? I think you should just forget about it and pretend you never saw the book.

I knew she was right. That book was trouble, but what else could I do? I replied to her,

"Babe, I really don't know what to think, but it's my job to investigate it. You can be sure a lot of people don't want this information made public. There are some very important names in there and I don't even know if any of it is true. The strangest thing is that they tried to take the body. One thing I know is that I have a job to do. Tomorrow is going to be one hell of a day and I'm sure Dr. Curphey will have something to say about the body being brought in."

Monday morning traffic was back to normal, bumper to bumper. The travel time was now over an hour, but it gave me time to reflect on what I had seen at the Hall of Justice. When I first came to the Coroner's Office in 1960, my responsibility was dealing with the public inquiries and keeping an up to date log on the status of open investigations. Now that I was a deputy, my responsibility was deeper.

The hot case of that time was George Reeves. Reeves, was the actor that played Superman in the hit television series, "The Adventures of Superman". Many people were unhappy with the ruling of "indicated suicide", in Reeves' death, including his mother, Helen Besselo, who was desperately trying to convince everyone her son had been murdered. She came in or called every week for a year to get Dr. Curphey to convene a Coroner's inquest or change his ruling of suicide.

Not sure how to handle the situation, I was sent to Dr. Curphey's office for an official briefing about the status of this sensitive case. Curphey was handling all inquiries for the Reeves death, and would advise me on how to answer her questions.

Dr. Curphey explained to me that Reeves' family had exhumed his body, and paid a pathologist for a second autopsy, while quickly commissioning their own investigation. Curphey said our official position was "the Coroner's Department was standing by its ruling, which is based on our autopsy findings and the Los Angeles Police Departments investigation." He added there would not be any inquest scheduled. Nevertheless, Mrs. Besselo called almost every day, and office personnel were advised to pass the calls along to me.

Her persistence led me to look through Reeves' official coroner files, where I discovered some interesting facts about his case. Apparently the deputy, who investigated the death, had been extremely quick to rule it a suicide. The police report said when they arrived, Reeves was lying naked on his bed, dead of a single gunshot wound to the right temple. The autopsy report indicated that there were no powder marks found on Reeves' body, and he had several fresh bruises.

Mrs Besselo told me that during their investigation, private detectives uncovered mountains of evidence that did not quite match up with the Coroner's ruling of suicide. Among some of the evidence uncovered was that no fingerprints were found on the gun. This left the possibility it was wiped clean. The spent shell casing was found underneath Reeves' body, which is very unusual, and the locations of the entrance and exit wounds did not line up with the path of the bullet. Its entrance into the wall indicated this.

Regardless of whether or not he killed himself, it was obvious that Reeves' death was never properly investigated. Private investigators were convinced that police detectives received pressured to make it an "open and shut" case.

In 1961, after I became a deputy, Dr. Curphey ordered Reeves' body exhumed and cremated without his mother's approval, forever destroying whatever evidence was left behind. When Mrs Besselo was informed and presented with the remains, she became highly depressed, dying a few years later.

This ordeal became my first experience involving an unsolved Hollywood mystery, but certainly was not the last. George Reeves, according to the official Coroner's findings, had committed suicide and the matter was closed.

Meanwhile, on the car radio, news of Monroe's death was on almost every station. As I got off the freeway, there seemed to be a lot of activity on the streets. In 1962, there were newspaper stands at every major intersection downtown. Men were coming up to cars, selling daily news. That morning they were screaming at the top of their lungs,

"Marilyn Monroe Found Dead!"

"Marilyn Monroe Commits Suicide!"

As I walked into the office that morning, it started to unfold in front of my very eyes. The normal laid back style of a somber Coroner's office was replaced by a frantic pace led by people who thought they were at the New York Stock Exchange. They were standing at the counter shouting things like, "Is Marilyn Monroe really here and can we view the body?"

Stiller was talking on the phone. He called out to me,

"Lionel, I'm glad you're here. I've got the New York Times on the phone, and they are asking if we are carrying her death as a homicide or suicide?"

I walked over to Phil Schwartzberg at the supervisor's

desk, and asked him had there been any up-dates. Phil said,

"We are waiting for word from the lab, but the police say suicide. Your job is getting her buried. We'll let the police handle the investigation."

After hanging up the phone, Stiller walked over and said,

"There were 2 men here about six this morning looking for you. They didn't identify themselves, but some of the guys from the autopsy room said they were Secret Service Agents. They were looking through some papers on your desk and for something in the medical department. Maybe some prescription bottles."

Although I couldn't determine what they were looking for on my desk, my thoughts went immediately to Marilyn's diary. After all, I had seen the President's name inside it. But how would they have known I had the diary? The only other person who saw it was Danbacker.

Apparently the Secret Service had also been in the autopsy room. Maybe they were there to question him and his partner about what they had recovered from the house. Not sure of what to think, I resumed my investigation, but the depth of the case was quickly becoming a reality.

I went over to Deputy Lester Goldberg's desk, who was the investigator that normally handled high profile cases. He had ten years investigating Coroner cases and all the contacts in the city. Goldberg wore tailor made suits, had a USC degree, and was said to have come from a well-connected family. People from around the country called him for official information from the Coroner office regarding complicated legal matters.

Goldberg was usually very well informed, so I asked him what he knew about Marilyn's case. He told me she was married to Joe DiMaggio and Arthur Miller, but wasn't sure if she was legally divorced. Goldberg said he was already in contact with Marilyn's lawyer and heard there was something strange about her death. He didn't want to discuss it right then, but emphasized we should go over it later, maybe during lunch.

Finally arriving to my desk, I discovered a note from, you guessed it, Dr. Curphey, who wanted to see me about Marilyn's case. Also the toxicology lab wanted more information from the physicians regarding prescription label discrepancies on the pill bottles Danbacker had brought in.

Walking down that long hall to Dr. Curphey's office was always an eerie experience. The sound of your shoe heels would echo like in a Hollywood horror movie. I was always anxious about meeting with Dr. Curphey. He was a big man who was very imposing and always had a frown on his face.

Highly respected in the pathology community, Curphey had a reputation for not caring what the public thought, or any one else for that matter. For that reason controversy seemed to follow him. He always seemed very mysterious and none of us employees at the Coroner's Department ever looked forward to being in his office. It usually meant we were receiving a lecture because he was unhappy with our work.

When I arrived, he was sitting at his desk with a man named Becker, his administrative assistant. Becker was second in command and oversaw all legal matters for the Coroner's office. As I walked in, it was obvious neither of them were happy. Curphey then sternly stated,

"Hope you realize the kind of pressure you put on this office with your rash decisions. This case shouldn't have been difficult because it was an obvious suicide. Now everybody is breathing down my neck for information and I don't need this crap. I'm assigning the Suicide Investigation Team to the case so get them anything they need. Let's bring this to a quick conclusion, understand?"

Having worked hard to get where I was, it was always very difficult for me to accept people speaking harshly to me. However, I simply nodded yes to Dr. Curphey and asked him if there would be an Inquest or a LAPD homicide investigation. Still speaking sternly, he replied, "No." I walked out of his office. Outside, there were 2 FBI officials waiting to see him. Having worked with them on several occasions, I nodded and went to the lab.

Dr. Ralph Abernathy was in charge of the Medical Department and responsible for toxicology, retrieving samples, conducting chemical test, and overseeing microscopic examinations. He had taken her first blood sample and found no poison or traces of other medication that Marilyn could have taken to contribute to her death. He advised me to send another deputy to her house and call the police to see if they had any information on other prescription containers at the scene.

Associated Press, United Press International, and the rest of the print media pool were still milling around the office looking for information regarding the case. Rumors were circulating among the reporters about Marilyn's death including whispers of Robert Kennedy's involvement and a press conference she had scheduled. Of course Marilyn Monroe was the hot topic around the office.

I hadn't released any information on what was in her property, like the diary or press release. There was a case to wrap-up and my investigation was still incomplete with pressure continuing to mount. I had Danbacker return to the house and bring back every prescription bottle he could find.

When I got back to my desk, I called Sergeant Jack Clemmons of the Los Angeles Police Department, who was the first officer at the scene. He informed me he was no longer on the case, but did give me some information on Marilyn's business agent, Imez Melson. I asked Sgt. Clemmons if he knew whom the current detectives in charge were, but he didn't know. This became a theme for the LAPD as her investigation went on. No one ever knew who was in charge of investigating this case.

When I contacted Melson, she said that Marilyn's mother, Gladys Pearl Monroe, was committed to a sanitarium with mental problems, and she didn't know of any other relatives. Melson also informed me that she thought there was a will.

Well it appeared as if only a will covering her estate or identifying someone that could handle her affairs would solve my problem. I pulled her property out and began to look for anything in the book that would reveal an executor. Truth be told, I wanted to take another look at her journal anyway, to see what information was really in there. This time I took notes.

CHAPTER 4:
The Little Red Book

The first 15 or 20 pages seemed to be recollections of her early involvement with specific people. These were long passages that took up full pages. As I began glancing through the journal, it became increasingly evident that Marilyn was involved in much more than movies. Page after page contained references to communist and different socio-political organizations. She was writing about intelligence agencies, using coded names and recounting some incredible experiences. The first thing I discovered was her relationship with the United States Government.

She wrote,

> *"The FBI wanted me to do something for America. They sent Iron Bob to ask me if Arthur was a Communist. When I told him we weren't that close he laughed and said you could get closer. He told me I should talk to Paula."*

According to her journal, Washington had recruited talent from far and wide for its crusade against Communism. During that time, I had no idea who Iron Bob or Paula was, but knew Marilyn had been married to Arthur Miller, that story was big news, and Lester Goldberg had reminded me about it earlier. However, it wasn't until years later I would discover these other identities.

As it turned out, Iron Bob would be later identified as Robert Maheu, an agent of the Federal Bureau of Investigation. Apparently he was the first to approach Marilyn. Maheu was a former World War II Super Spy, who had posed as a Nazi sympathizer during the war. He also contracted with the Central Intelligence Agency doing assignments when the agency could not officially be involved.

Paula was discovered to be actor Lee Strasberg's wife. She was also Marilyn's acting coach. Paula Strasberg had been blacklisted as a Communist by the Government, and apparently had some type of connection with the Bureau. According to FBI disclosures, Maheu was very effective in setting up covert operations such as this. It seems Maheu asked Marilyn to get information on Arthur Miller's alleged communist activities and Strasberg coached her through the process.

According to Marilyn, Maheu was keeping record of Miller's social and political activities. Apparently, there was an ongoing investigation into his association with groups making public statements against the government and its anti-communist blacklist.

She wrote,

"Iron Bob wanted the names of people with us during social engagements and information on Arthur's meetings with the American Labor Party and the ACLU."

Even during my younger years, I was always very socially and politically conscious. My grandparents were among the first African-American homeowners in the San Fernando Valley of Southern California. My grandfather was a Military veteran, construction worker and part of the Union movement in the African-American and Latino communities.

Seeing Marilyn write about these highly charged subjects fascinated me. Was it really possible that this blonde-bombshell Hollywood starlet was involved with these types of activities? Coincidently or not, Marilyn Monroe's movie career suddenly went into another gear during this time.

On New Year's Eve 1955, Marilyn signed a new contract with 20th Century Fox Studios to make four films over a seven-year period. She formed Marilyn Monroe Productions, which would be paid $100,000, plus a share of profits for each film.

In addition to being able to work for other studios, Monroe had the right to reject any script, director, or cinematographer she did not approve of. Before signing this deal, Marilyn's typical pay for a movie was only about $18,000.

We know that Hollywood was reeling with investigations by the House Un American Activities Committee into certain actors and writers. When the government accused you of being a Communist in the motion picture business, your ability to get a job or finance a film went downhill, but if they needed your help, sky was the limit. With this power, it would have been easy for the FBI to get Studios to cooperate in their investigation, sign Marilyn to a lucrative new deal and cast her in some key roles.

Marilyn wrote in-depth pages about Arthur Miller and how the FBI was playing a central role early in their relationship. Iron Bob's name occurred repeatedly in this part of her writings.

Later she wrote,

> *"After we were married, Arthur said he wanted me to go to Russia with him. It sounded exciting but when Iron Bob got wind of it, he told me I was getting in too deep."*

Why was Iron Bob concerned about Marilyn getting in too deep? Was he apprehensive about her relationship with Miller? Later, I learned according to F.B.I records, Miller did ask her to go to the Soviet Embassy and apply for a visa. He wanted her to get a first hand look at what the socialists were all about. The fact that the government knew Miller had asked Marilyn to go give credence to her accounts in the book.

Arthur Miller was one of the nation's leading activists, who had recently written a Broadway play called "The Crucible" which was produced as a statement against McCarthyism, when the US government blacklisted accused communists. During that time, the U.S. House of Representatives had an investigative branch called the House Un-American Activities Committee. They were targeting and blacklisting writers who had written controversial books and screenplays about America. Miller was subpoenaed to appear in front of the committee.

On one page I saw,

"Paula and Lee told Arthur to come clean with the Committee but he said he would not sell out his friends. Don't know why I gave that information. Guess I could be considered a sell out."

Apparently, just before his appearance in front of the House Un-American Activities Committee, Lee and Paula Strasberg had suggested that he go as a "friendly" witness, something that Paula herself had done several years earlier.

It seemed as though Marilyn began to second-guess her role in gathering information for the FBI. I don't think she ever thought it would be used in court against Miller. My belief is that Maheu and Strasberg convinced Marilyn they were investigating other people and organizations. However, the House Un-American Activities Committee still subpoenaed Miller.

Arthur Miller was found guilty of contempt of Congress for not naming some suspected communist writers whom he had met with.

Marilyn wrote,

"The war against communism tore our industry apart. I'm sorry they used me to get him."

I remember visiting Los Angeles City College in the late 50's, while preparing to enroll, and being surprised to see so many communist activities around the campus. Most of the groups were professional students, a little older than the average student. They gave parties, passed out reading material, and had what was called Head Sessions where everyone sat around and talked politics.

The main topic was the federal government's illegal persecution of American citizens and socialist heroes. Some of the favorite subjects were Leon Trotsky and Arthur Miller. In the late 1950's, Miller was a hero to non conformist around the world. His Contempt of Congress conviction for failing to give names to the Committee mobilized the movement temporarily, but had turned Hollywood into a paranoid community.

This was an international headline, but the biggest story in the newspapers was at the trial. One of the Congressional Committee members said he would vote to drop the case if Marilyn would pose in a picture with him. Arthur Miller said no thanks. I did not see a comment by Marilyn on this.

I had seen television accounts and news clips which showed Marilyn at his side at various court appearances. After Miller's conviction had been overturned by the Court of Appeals, he was really upset that as a condition of the dismissal, the Committee was urging him to write something less tragic about America.

Government officials encouraged Miller to begin work on *The Misfits*, which was to star Marilyn and an aging American box office icon named Clark Gable.

After many heated conversations between Marilyn and Miller, concerning the screenplay, shooting commenced on *The Misfits*. She had envisioned it as containing a serious dramatic role for her without the sexual implications. She knew the language of House Committee and how she wanted to be portrayed.

The production did not go smoothly and it became her last completed film. Directed by John Huston and co-starring Clark Gable, Montgomery Clift, and Eli Wallach, *The Misfits* opened to mixed reviews. During the filming, public arguments about the dialogue between the Strasbergs and Miller were reported by the press.

As I continued to scribble down points of interest, a very interesting name began to appear on the pages, Psychiatrist Dr. Ralph Greenson. He was one of the doctors who had reported Marilyn death.

She wrote,

"Frank introduced me to Doctor Greenson. He was able to get me some pills that relaxed me. I wondered if Frank knew Greenson was a party member."

Later she wrote,

"Dr. Greenson spent hours with me discussing world politics. It reminded me about some of the talks I had with Arthur."

Doctor Ralph Greenson would play a major role in the events that would transpire during the final year of Marilyn's life. No foreign policy issue was more sensitive than Cuba and its Russian allies in the early sixties. Anything Marilyn passed on to Dr. Greenson concerning what the Kennedy's said privately would have breached National Security.

There wasn't nearly enough time to read all that was in this journal, yet I continued thumbing through the diary looking for leads. She had written so much. The notes I was taking were just snapshots of the stories she was describing. Something to help me remember what she had wrote about. Familiar names and organizations equally caught my attention.

The next entry I read was about her relationship with the President of the United States, John F. Kennedy.

Marilyn wrote,

"The best day of my life. I met Jack at Peter's house. He was introduced as Senator John Kennedy and the next president of the United States. I wanted to stay calm but he was so exciting. His confidence, intelligence, and charm struck me. It lit a fire. We started seeing each other."

Her reference to Jack kind of threw me, but this was John Kennedy's nickname. Over the next few pages, it was apparent that Marilyn became involved with John Kennedy. There were graphic accounts of their relationship as she recalled "Kinky" parties they attended. Marilyn seemed to enjoy that lifestyle. Although she was still married to Arthur Miller at this time, according to her notes, she was constantly in the company of John Kennedy.

She penned all of these entries,

"The thing with Jack was getting hot. I love all that real life drama. Just think I'm in on it."

"Got to see Jack every time he came to New York City. I was close to Arthur and working regularly too."

"I was with the next President and we made violent love."

She drew a couple of cartoons after that entry. The biggest one was a happy face.

After John Kennnedy was elected to President, Marilyn divorced Miller and soon after began in earnest the last phase of her life. She started attending meetings in New York with JFK and members of the Central Intelligence Agency or as she called them, the Spy Boys. It wasn't clear if she was taking part in these discussions or just window dressing.

She wrote about one of the meetings.

"The spy boys were really serious about killing Castro. Big Jim and a guy named Eduardo were actually involved in the Bay of Pigs. Jack never let them forget it."

The Bay of Pigs had been a big CIA disaster in Cuba during the early months of Kennedy's administration. With the support of the US Government, a CIA-trained force attempted to invade southern Cuba in an effort to overthrow Fidel Castro. The invasion was launched in April 1961, less than three months after John F. Kennedy assumed the presidency. The Cuban armed forces easily defeated the invading combatants within three days.

It was quite interesting to see Marilyn writing about the Bay of Pigs. That incident was a very intense time for many Americans. However, decades would pass before I would discover the identity of the two men she mentioned in that entry. The Big Jim she was talking about was Jim O'Connell, a CIA operative documented as being in charge of the Agency's Castro Assassination plot at that time.

O'Connell and President Kennedy were meeting to adopt the plan to assassinate Fidel Castro with Marilyn looking on. Eduardo, who she had mentioned, was none other than Howard Hunt of Watergate fame. Hunt was the head of Kennedy's covert operations in Cuba. Apparently, the highest level of information gathering and clandestine activities was being formulated at these meetings.

While reading Marilyn's diary, I made notes of three separate meetings she attended with Central Intelligence Agents. In recent years, Congressional disclosures have verified her accounts of these conversations. At some of the meetings, she noted that Mafia high rollers, Sam Giancana and Johnny Roselli were also in attendance. Her writings disclosed that Roselli discussed a previous attempt to assassinate Castro.

She said of that meeting,

> *"We attended a meeting with the spy boys and mafia gangsters. They were discussing how to kill Castro. Johnny Roselli boasted about the Mafia's ability to infiltrate anybody's security to kill them. They had a pill to cram up Castro's butt."*

A later CIA document quoted Roselli, saying a Cuban with Mafia ties tried to mix the pill in Castro's drink, but got cold feet. He also said the CIA provided a suppository that could be put in a person's rectum. Were these tools of the trade a clue as to how Marilyn was killed?

I could never tell if she interacted with all these officials or their underworld associates. She wrote what she thought about the meetings and conversations, but didn't give a clue regarding her participation. One thing was certain; Marilyn was involved not only with the White House, FBI and CIA, but some of the most dangerous gangsters of that time.

With knowledge of secret American attempts to overthrow at least two foreign governments and the President's association with Mafia figures, Marilyn found herself right in the middle of world politics. I couldn't help, but think to myself, "So have I."

Regardless of everything, it was apparent that part of Marilyn enjoyed the intrigue and interaction that came with the CIA. They had began to take up a great deal of her time, which showed in her writtings. Her topics changed from killing Castro to other clandestine activities.

She made these entries about her activities with the CIA.

"Big Jim wanted me to do a job for them. They were trying to bring down a foreign leader, who doesn't want to cooperate."

"Bob and Big Jim talked about shooting a film with Howard Hughes to embarrass this diplomat."

"Bob said we were going to see Mr. Hughes to set it up."

It took a little time for these pages to make sense to me, but I knew Howard Hughes was one the richest men in the world. What I didn't know was that Hughes was also the government's largest contractor.

Hughes had introduced one of Hollywood's more controversial films when he released "The Outlaw". The production featured one of Marilyn's friends, Jane Russell, who defied the set standard of morally acceptable content in motion pictures by showcasing her breasts. Terry Moore, another one of Marilyn's friends, had also been married to Hughes.

Hughes and Robert Maheu formed a partnership that participated in CIA activities regularly. The foreign leader in question was Indonesian President Achmad Sukarno, who was deemed to be communist influenced by the CIA.

Big Jim O'Connell had been promoted to Chief of Far East Operations. He remembered Marilyn and knew she could assist him with this high-level assignment.

Marilyn wrote,

> *"They set up photo ops at a couple of hotels and when the diplomat came to visit Jack, he was seen with me."*

Marilyn apparently had also spent some time in Mexico. She wrote about a meeting with the Fair Play for Cuba Committee.

> *"At the meeting, I heard the Cubans were being pushed into the Soviet Bloc by American policy. They love Castro. I don't think Big Jim will ever get him."*

Later, I found out the senior FBI official in Mexico had taken notice and sent Director J. Edgar Hoover a four-page report. It said that Monroe had associated closely with certain members of the American Communist Group and visited the Cuban and Soviet Union Embassies.

One of the people she was accused of associating with was identified by the CIA as a person of interest in a Cuban missile deployment file. His name was deleted from FBI disclosures. One of this man's companions at the Cuban and Soviet Embassies was a man who would later waltz into the history books, Lee Harvey Oswald.

Marilyn never mentioned either man's name in the book, but the possibility exists of them crossing paths. I can't imagine a steady trail of American tourist with CIA ties visiting these embassies. However, this common denominator of English speaking people in a Spanish speaking country would be enough for a chance meeting.

FBI Director Hoover labeled Marilyn a national security risk. Many have speculated on why she was in Mexico City. Perhaps this memo helped cover-up what her real motives were. Whatever information Marilyn gathered while she was at the Embassy's or in private conversations has never been disclosed, but I'm sure the data is in some file maintained by a federal agency.

The diary might have had more information, but there just was not enough time to read the details more thoroughly. This trip did appear to be much more than it seemed and, as the years passed I came to believe that it might have seriously impacted Marilyn's life and death.

In 1962, I had no real idea as to what this diary meant, but it was easy to understand how documenting these events could pose a problem. Marilyn was involved not only with the White House and Organized Crime, but the CIA's overthrow of foreign governments. Now, after her trip to Mexico City, she was also considered a security risk by the FBI.

Apparently J. Edgar Hoover was concerned about Marilyn's relationship with the Kennedy's. In a memo released under the Freedom of Information Act, he discussed a meeting and conversation on world politics Marilyn had with John Kennedy at actor Peter Lawford's house. How could he have known what they discussed? Did Hoover have Lawford's house tapped?

I began to realize that her public perception as a dumb blond in her films and her sex goddess image seemed superficial in comparison to this well written expose'. It told the story of a seemingly complicated existence. Marilyn had been thrust into an environment that she had no control over. I believe she had gotten in deeper than anybody ever realized and according to her writings things began to unravel.

She stated,

"My life was very confusing after Jack became President. I wanted to go to

the White House all dressed up like when I met the Queen but I wasn't his damn wife. That was so depressing."

In 1962, as news of her affair with the President began to be discussed in Washington, her now famous appearance in New York seemingly was the straw that broke the camel's back.

"Peter asked me to sing Happy Birthday during Jack's party at Madison Square Garden. I finally met his brother Bobby. It was fun but didn't work out."

Although her "Happy Birthday Mr. President" performance made big headlines, it was not a particularly good night for Marilyn. The First Lady, Jackie Kennedy, was there along with the rest of the family. Years later, I spoke with Marilyn's friend, Jeanne Carmine, who told me that someone had threatened Marilyn not to show up that night. Jackie was aware of her affair with JFK, and had confronted him about it.

However, the most interesting part about the entry was Marilyn mentioning meeting Bobby Kennedy for first time. Bobby was the Attorney General then and I was very familiar with him. About a year earlier, he had delivered a powerful radio broadcast for Voice of America, defending America's record on race relations to the rest of the world.

When I first heard him give that address, I remember thinking how idealistic he sounded. Bobby Kennedy had passion and struck me as someone who cared about the struggles of Black people.

During that time, the Freedom Riders was the talk of the African-American community. Both Kennedy brothers had taken that opportunity to begin building a rapport with civil rights leaders. A great many of the initiatives that occurred during the Kennedy Administration were a result of the passion and determination of Robert Kennedy, who underwent a thorough conversion of purpose as their relationship expanded.

In September 1961, Bobby Kennedy requested the Interstate Commerce Commission to make rules banning all segregated seating in interstate terminals and vehicles.

This ruling gave the Freedom Riders an unequivocal victory in their campaign. Students from all over the country purchased bus tickets to the South and crowded into jails in Jackson, Mississippi. With the participation of northern students, even more press coverage transpired, and as more people in the U.S. learned about the Freedom Riders, the more they wanted to support them.

The country felt bad about the unnecessary violence and lack of police protection for the Freedom Riders, which embarrassed the United States on the world stage.

Seeing Bobby's name in Marilyn's writings was as

surprising as anything I had seen up to this point. Never could I have imagined what his role would be in this case and subsequent cover-up.

As I continued flipping through the pages, I began to notice something else. It was beginning to become more difficult to ascertain whether Marilyn was writing about past or current events. One thing was very certain; things had not been going well since the President's birthday party.

This very impassioned entry would follow,

"Jack stopped taking my calls. He even had the nerve to change his phone number. Peter told me Jackie was raising hell and would divorce him if he ever saw me again. Wish she had left him. I could have been his wife. I'm not afraid of these aristocrats."

This was a long page, something she had not written since earlier parts of the book. Kennedy apparently yielded to his wife's demand and that's when Bobby's name began to appear frequently on the pages. Evidence suggests that John sent his brother to explain why he couldn't see her again. Now if John lit a fire inside Marilyn, Bobby was like a nuclear explosion. According to her diary she fell head over heals in love with him.

After that, her tone seemed to change. When she began

writing again, it was a more serious Marilyn that emerged. It was as though she stopped looking back and was documenting the moments. There were notations of days and dates on some pages. Without a doubt she was now keeping an account of her current activities.

I made note of a meeting she attended with Bobby Kennedy.

"Big meeting in San Diego. Jim was there and Bobby was glad to see him. I love being with Bobby. He say's we're going to make America the most powerful country in the world."

For 10 pages or so, Bobby and Marilyn were acting like teenage lovers. The entries were steamy with conversations of love and marriage on almost every page. The way she described it gave me the impression of this being a very happy time of her life.

Although the book was captivating, so far none of it was offering any real assistance to finding a next of kin. Wanting a second opinion about the book, I walked over to Lester Goldberg's desk and asked him if we were still on for lunch. He told me to give him a minute, and then we went to grab a bite.

As we sat down to eat, Lester told me he had received some very high-level phone calls about Marilyn's case. He said,

"They're asking some pretty strange questions about our investigation and it seems like they're looking for something. All of it is very unusual."

I pulled the book out and told him this had arrived with her property. Showing him some of the entries, Goldberg knew this book would be something of interest to the press and federal authorities. He said,

"This information could be used by anyone with a bone to pick with the Kennedy's. I'm glad it's your case, because I don't want investigators asking me about this hot potato. Good luck finding what you need, but you better be careful. I'll let you know if I hear anything else."

When I got back from lunch, the paperwork from my workload was beginning to pile up. After making a few phone calls, I tried gathering some information for my other cases. Armand came to me with the preliminary toxicology report. This test would disclose what was in the blood, and they did not find much. There was no poison in the stomach, presenting the possibility she had not ingested any pills. We looked at each other, and then I asked him,

"Did you check with the medical department if this is true?

Armand nodded yes and said,

"Abernathy has sent out the samples for further microscopic examination. You better make out some kind of statement for the press."

The examination would take 4 to 6 weeks and we would

need a medical determination before I could request Dr. Curphey to order a full police investigation, or at least a coroner's inquest.

Dr. Thomas Noguchi had been assigned the autopsy, and he was the best the County had to offer. He was a no nonsense kind of guy, whose professionalism made our job a little easier when dealing with medical questions from the family. Having a doctor there made things contentious, and he was the only one who would take the time to explain a cause of death to family members or the Coroner's representative who was on the case. Most of the other Autopsy Surgeons did not want anything to do with the family, press, or the police.

I went to the autopsy room to see if there was anything he needed from our unit for the autopsy. When I arrived, Dr. Noguchi was in the room talking to Deputy District Attorney John Miner, who was scheduled to be present at Marilyn's autopsy. Miner was a liaison between the District Attorney's medical legal section and the Coroner's office. He carried medical information, personal identification certifications and personal property between our office and theirs. Miner visited us often and we had worked together several times in the past. The fact that he was going to present at the autopsy showed the District Attorney's office had a special interest in the case.

Marilyn's body was lying on the gurney, covered by a sheet and being prepared for the autopsy. Miner and

Noguchi were looking at some bruises on her leg. I could clearly see a bruise just below the knee. Dr. Noguchi was explaining that this was common because many people fall or the body is bruised when being handled after death. I wasn't a doctor, but this didn't look like a bruise from a fall. Besides, wasn't she was found dead on a bed? My first thought was needle mark, but obviously Dr. Noguchi didn't concur.

Something else was bothering me. Why was Deputy District Attorney Miner in the autopsy room a day before the autopsy? He was scheduled to witness Dr. Noguchi perform it the following morning at 8:00am. This was extremely irregular, particularly in a non-homicide investigation.

Not wanting to disturb them, I told Dr. Noguchi to let me know if he needed anything for the autopsy and decided to check back with Deputy Danbacker to see what he found at the house. Danbacker had been with the Coroner's office for a couple of years. He was an immigrant European and spoke with a very thick accent. Nobody at the office could pronounce his first name, so we all called him Danbacker.

He told me the house had been completely cleaned and there weren't any prescription containers or medication anywhere. I asked him to tell me what he saw when he picked up the body the day before, hoping he could shed a little light on things.

The Deputy told me she was found dead in her bedroom but because of the discoloration, it was easy to see the body had been moved. He also reiterated that she had died much earlier, because rigor mortis had already begun to set in. When the final physical diagram and autopsy report was completed, no mention of these details, or the bruise marks on her body, were reported.

I returned to my desk and just sat there a moment. My head was literally spinning from this investigation. Nothing was making any sense and on top of everything else there was that crazy diary. I looked at my pages of messy notes, which had no executor, no next of kin, or any indication of who should be responsible for her burial.

Time was running short. By then, I had already concluded there would be no executor listed in this book, but it no longer mattered. My investigation had taken a completely different turn. The more I tried to make sense of the strange circumstances surrounding her death, the more I was convinced something was very wrong. First somebody tries to remove the body from the house, now no poison is found in her stomach, yet everybody is still yelling suicide.

All I could do was keep reading on. Marilyn began describing detailed accounts of her encounters with Bobby Kennedy. She wrote about his fierce courtroom battle with Jimmy Hoffa, which was covered intensely by the media.

She wrote,

"Bobby was on the phone most of the night talking to Jack. It was

something about putting that guy Hoffa in jail."

In recalling the writings, I never had the feeling that she was a frantic woman and her descriptions seemed well thought out. It was plain to see why she was consciously writing it down. She was subconsciously trying to process the information.

But things began to change. Marilyn wanted more from her relationship with Bobby Kennedy. According to Jeanne Carmine, she heard Marilyn on the phone at her house telling him to leave his wife on more than one occasion. But he was Catholic and a divorce would surely destroy his political career.

She wrote,

"I asked Bobby again about us. He told me don't be ridiculous. Said he was going to become President after Jack and I'm not going to ruin it."

For the first time, I began to see a sense of desperation on the pages. In the beginning, she had described almost everything in detail, sometimes taking 2 or 3 pages. Now everything was short and to the point. On one particular page she described another interaction with Kennedy.

Someone had apparently told him that she was keeping notes on their activities. Bobby confronted Marilyn about the book.

> *"Bobby found out about my diary. Can't believe he raised holy hell for writing about us. Told me to destroy it. Never thought he would react like that."*

Marilyn's dream of a future with Bobby Kennedy began falling apart. Her passages became shorter and angrier as she began to realize the truth of her situation.

> *"Couldn't reach Bobby and he won't call back."*

> *"The dirty bastard changed his number. He thinks he going to do me like his brother did. I'll fix them all."*

I put the diary back down and grabbed the press release on my desk. Marilyn apparently had scheduled a press conference that Tuesday, according to the press release that was in her purse. Topic: "Marilyn Reveals it All."

Was this book what she had planned to disclose? Although my understanding of what Marilyn was saying wasn't clear, I knew that if she talked to the press about what she had written, the country was in for a shock.

It was around three o'clock by then and some other cases

still needed closing out before going home. I picked up the diary and thumbed down towards the end of the book.

Marilyn's desperation became even more evident. She seemed to have much more of an 'I don't care' attitude, and her next several entries reflected that feeling.

She wrote,

"Frank called tonight, maybe I'll go to Tahoe and let my hair down."

On the final weekend in July, Marilyn flew to Lake Tahoe, Nevada for an exclusive Frank Sinatra party. According to her personal accounts, she met Teamster Leader Jimmy Hoffa, who was there with Mafia boss Sam Giancana.

She wrote,

"I met Jimmy Hoffa at Frank's party. Made a big fool of myself. Drank too much and smoked too much. Sam and him were asking about Bobby. What did I say?"

The next couple of pages were intense, as Marilyn struggled to cope with her and Bobby's relationship. In some cases, her writings were incoherent, as if she were drunk or using drugs.

She wrote about a phone call.

"Peter called. Bobby is coming tomorrow. They want me to call off the press conference. Too late."

Peter Lawford and Bobby Kennedy knew about the press conference. But what did that prove? Would they have killed her for that? I kept reading. She went on to describe the first of two hostile visits by Kennedy.

"Bobby was really mad. Acted crazy and searched all my stuff. Told him it's mine. I'll never let him have it."

The second visit was later that evening, according to neighbors who saw Robert Kennedy and Peter Lawford enter the house.

She wrote,

"Bobby came back with Peter. Shook me until I was dizzy and threw me on the bed. Should call the doctor."

That was the last coherent entry Marilyn made in her diary. There was no doubt her last accounts were more relevant to her death. I flipped through the final pages glancing at the writing. It seemed as though she had become detached and the entries weren't legible. There was obviously something wrong.

I really didn't know what to make of what I had just

read. Bobby Kennedy had an altercation with Marilyn over this diary. There was no date on this entry so it was difficult to establish the time between when this was written and when she died. But I had to ask myself, was this the final night?

In my mind there were more questions than answers about this journal, diary, or whatever it was. I decided to turn the book over to Dr. Curphey, but he was already gone. Thinking Lester may have discovered something new, I walked over to see him, he had left as well. After spending the entire day dealing with this case, talking to investigators, gathering paperwork, answering phone calls, and of course reading the diary, I just wanted to put everything away and go home too.

Dr. Noguchi had scheduled the autopsy for the next morning. So I straightened out my desk, took the diary, and locked it in the safe with the rest of her property. With Tuesday and Wednesday off, a short vacation from the Coroner's Office sounded like just what the doctor ordered. The preliminary autopsy report would be ready when I got back and that was going to tell a big part of the story. I grabbed my notes and left. I needed to wrap my head around the events of the past two days.

CHAPTER 5:
The Cover-Up

Visions of the Kennedy's, FBI, CIA, Castro, and Jimmy Hoffa were dancing around in my head as I drove home. Marilyn Monroe had been working for the Federal Bureau of Investigation and Central Intelligence Agency. These were two of the most powerful organizations in the world. The CIA, who most Americans knew little about during that time, was formed when Congress passed the National Security Act in 1947, replacing the Office of Strategic Services as America's spy agency and intelligence-gathering group.

Although America's elected officials funded the agency, the general public didn't know or want to know what they were doing. I knew nothing about the Central Intelligence Agency, but was a fan of CBS Network News. That kept me reasonably informed for political conversations around the office. But these subjects are not what I talked about with my friends.

Television broadcasts and major market newspapers were the only sources of national news. The only way you could find out about this secretive group was to have someone write about them or on a television newscast. As I found out later, journalism was a perfect cover for CIA agents. People talk freely to journalists, and few thought suspiciously of a journalist aggressively asking questions or searching for information.

Not surprisingly, the CIA had begun a mission to recruit American journalists on a wide scale. They wanted these journalists not only to relay any sensitive information they had discovered, but also write anti-communist, pro-capitalist, and pro CIA propaganda when needed. In the 1950s, some 3,000 people were contracted and paid by the CIA to further its policies. Many of them would be used for this cover-up.

On the other hand, their counterparts, the Federal Bureau Of Investigation, and its Director, J. Edgar Hoover had a broad reputation for dealing with crime and communism. There were films and television shows about them and they were presented as being all that was good in America.

Some of the harshest criticism of Hoover, and the FBI, was spying on elected officials. Their Counter Intelligence Program, also known as COINTELPRO, was notorious for disrupting the Communist Party, and later, organizations such as the Black Panther Party and Martin Luther King Jr.'s Southern Christian Leadership Conference.

Their methods included infiltration, burglaries, illegal wiretaps, planting forged documents, and spreading false rumors about key members of target organizations. Trying to understand Marilyn's involvement in all this was nearly impossible. As I crept along through the Monday evening traffic, I was just glad the day was over.

It always felt good coming home to the sanity of my family. Along with my wife and three kids, we lived at a house located in Pacoima, 15 miles north of downtown Los Angeles. It was an integrated working class neighborhood where everybody knew each other.

My wife was overwhelmed by the depth of Marilyn's writings after glancing through the names and far-reaching details of the notes. When I told her how the press would love to have this information, she advised me to throw my notes away.

Her mother, who worked as a stenographer for the Los Angeles Police Department, agreed. I remember what she told me,

"Your family is the number 1 priority. You've got a job most colored men would love to have. Why would you slander the Kennedy's when it looks like they are going to do something good for this country? The Police Department will handle it."

I never liked being called a Colored, but I understood what they were saying. Besides, it was never my intention to let anyone else see my notes. My mother in law and her sister were dedicated civil service employees. They were trailblazers in City and County Government, active in local politics, and worked on various Ad-Hoc political Committees. I asked my Mother in law what she thought about J. Edgar Hoover and she said,

"The FBI is our last line of defense if we want law and order especially now that we want civil and voting rights. They are doing what has to be done"

Her son and her sister's husband were both Teamsters with whom I had many conversations about Jimmy Hoffa. I asked them that evening what did they know about the Hoffa-Kennedy feud. They contended that Kennedy represented the super rich and he had it in for the Union, even though they had voted in great numbers for his brother. Both of them were giving total support to Hoffa against anybody.

I regularly had breakfast with them at some of the truck driver eateries in downtown Los Angeles. One of our favorite spots was the Original Pantry on 9th and Figueroa. On any given weekday morning, you could get a big slice of Americana just by dropping in there. If there were any doubts about the solidarity of these unions, it would have quickly been dismissed once you were around them.

Their main concern was job security and wages for their families. The auto and aircraft workers were also in total support of their union's efforts. They represented the emerging middle class environment that was taking the nation by storm and their strength was at the ballot box.

Reading Marilyn's diary helped to reshape my notion of reality, opening my eyes to a different aspect of our society. Her accounts of involvement with the White House and other powerful government agencies provided me with new insight into our Nation's Foreign and Domestic Policy.

The people she wrote about were leading America's efforts in Nuclear Weapons proliferation, International plots in Indonesia and other key domestic issues such as Communism, Civil Rights, Labor, and Employment. Marilyn's diary raised serious questions about how political figures and Government Agencies were attempting to shape the lives of people around the world. It forced me to do the research necessary for an inside look at what Marilyn had written and the people that she had written about. I needed to know if it was true, and what it all meant.

Things were a little eerie for the next few days with strange cars driving up and down the street slowly. This became so obvious that one of my neighbors walked out and approached a car parked in front of her house. When she asked the two men sitting inside who were they looking for, they just drove off. In our neighborhood, strangers only meant the police or a repo man. I never knew who they were, but they weren't just door-to-door salesmen.

While mowing the lawn on Wednesday morning, I noticed two peculiar cars driving slowly down the street. They were four door official looking cars with nothing to indicate who they were or where they came from. I looked at them and they looked at me. With all this activity, everybody had the feeling something was wrong.

After we discussed it, one of my neighbors suggested we call the police. My wife was a good ambassador and she kept the emotions down, although I knew what she was thinking. Neither of us was sure if this was about the diary, and we didn't say a word. It would have been embarrassing for our neighbors to know these people were possibly watching me.

That night, as my wife and I watched the evening news, we saw coverage of Marilyn's Funeral. Apparently Joe DiMaggio finally had agreed to handle her arrangements. As we both sat there, quietly looking at the service, somehow I felt connected to Marilyn, and found myself more determined than ever to learn the truth about her death.

Needless to say, there were a lot of things on my mind when I came back to work. After two days off, my desk was a mess, and nobody even took time to stack the new paperwork neatly. Everything was out of order, like someone was looking for something every so often.

Besides the new cases that were assigned to me, there was a stack of inquiries about the status of Marilyn's case. The preliminary results of the autopsy had arrived, showing no trace of any medication she was taking. None of the drugs from the empty prescription containers brought in were discovered in her blood.

Dr. Noguchi had found 30 Nembutal tablets lodged in her throat. Dr. Abernathy had requested further microscopic examination because the first test was inconclusive.

Well, I immediately thought that would destroy the suicide angle. If she had attempted to take her life by filling her mouth with pills, then she had failed. I called Noguchi to ask if this lab report would change the status of the case. He said no, because they were ordering additional test on the tissues and the liver.

There was still no preliminary police report. Deputy Goldberg came over to my desk and said he had something for me. He stated,

"An Associated Press reporter told him that Robert Kennedy is somehow involved in this. His sources are saying that he was in the house the night she died."

Lester stood there, looking me directly in my eyes and said,

"Lionel, be careful because there is a gathering of eagles hovering over this particular case. LAPD and the FBI are crawling all over the city looking for some important evidence. Cover your butt."

Lester was always saying things like that, but there was something much more serious about this. He looked nervous, even scared, and that wasn't like him. Those words, however, turned out to be prophetic. The eagles did begin to circle around my head, and I didn't have my hat on.

Dr. Curphey had issued a statement that he wanted all

information about the Monroe case, coming in or going out, cleared with him. I decided there was no choice but to inform him about the diary. I went to retrieve it from the safe, and discovered it had been removed. I grabbed the sign out sheet to see who took it, but there was no record of the book's removal. In fact, everything was gone.

I reported the missing property to Phil Schwartzberg, my supervising deputy, and Richard Rathbun, my department head. Rathbun was a forty-year county employee who followed Dr. Curphey's instructions to the letter. He was one of only three people who had his own office within the Coroner's department, and had keys to every important lock. When I informed them about her property, they seemed unconcerned and told me the contents would turn up.

Their response was surprising to me because of Dr. Curphey's explicit orders regarding evidence in this case. However, there was nothing I could do or say about it, so I simply went on with my other duties. Maybe they knew what had happened to it and didn't want to tell me, but there was no way of knowing. I couldn't help but ask myself though, how many other people found out about the book while I had been away from the office?

After returning to my desk, Armand came over and said Marilyn's press agent, Pat Newcomb, had came into the office, while I was off and asked about what was in Marilyn's property. Armand said he looked in the safe, but nothing was there and the log sheet said nothing. He mentioned that he spoke to Lester, who told him I had it on Monday. Amazed at his timing, I told him her property was missing and my thoughts were that Dr. Curphey probably had it.

After I thought about it, Deputy Danbacker and Deputy Goldberg were the only ones who knew about Marilyn's articles being at the Coroner's Office. There was no reason for anybody else to be looking through her property, unless they were looking for something specifically.

Since her property had not been signed out, it was logical to assume that Dr. Curphey had it in his possession. One thing was for sure; whoever took her property out of the safe would have seen the explosive nature of Marilyn's diary. By now, some government agency or police department official may have looked in it. The White House certainly would have had an interest, and I know the Secret Service was looking around that Sunday morning. There was also a flip side. What if it got into the wrong hands? There could be far reaching ramifications.

Although Marilyn's funeral had occurred the day before, her body remained the property of the Los Angeles County Coroner. The Public Administrator, Baldo Kristovich had allowed her body to be released for the funeral service, however it was to be returned to the morgue pending a next of kin ruling. The final part of this investigation was gathering all medical data, including toxicology reports and autopsy results, along with the additional police information needed to close this complicated case.

The public was wondering why Marilyn was still in the County morgue. They called over 200 times a day with questions about her death. True to his word, Dr. Curphey had assigned the infamous Suicide Investigation Team to research the evidence. He appointed Dr. Robert Littman, a psychiatrist, and Dr. Norman Farberow, a psychologist, to probe the case. They were a pair of doctors from a Los Angeles Suicide Prevention Organization, and were commissioned to find out everything about Marilyn's personal life. After concluding an investigation, they would submit an official report stating, in their professional opinion, whether she was a likely candidate for suicide.

My supervisor, Deputy Schwartzberg, asked me to work with the team that morning to arrange a press conference. Dr. Curphey wanted to assure the country that the team would interview, under oath, everyone who could shed light on her death. He said the press release should include a statement saying the Coroner would guarantee a thorough investigation, utilizing their subpoena power for witnesses, and calling for an inquest if necessary.

Schwartzberg told me the Los Angeles Police Department was under extreme pressure from Washington to close their case, and so were we. He said we shouldn't expect LAPD to provide any further reports on the circumstances and to proceed without them.

He was true to what he said. Over the next week, I must have called 20 or so times to access a police investigation report, without success. However, something else strange had happened. Rumors were circulating around the office that someone from the D.A.'s office didn't believe Marilyn had committed suicide.

Trying to get more information, I went to see what Lester Goldberg knew. He told me that Deputy District Attorney John Miner had sent a memo to Dr. Curphey about the autopsy, and about an interview he did with Dr. Ralph Greenson. Miner said Greenson told him Marilyn wasn't suicidal. Lester said, "Curphey's not budging."

That same day, I was told to arrange another press conference, this time announcing the conclusion of the Suicide Investigation Team's findings. It was difficult to believe these doctors could complete their analysis so quickly, but I scheduled the press conference.

On August 17, 1962, Dr. Curphey made this statement to press members from around the world:

Statement by Theodore J. Curphey, M.D.
Chief Medical Examiner-Coroner
County of Los Angeles

Now that the final toxicological report and that of the psychiatric consultants have been received and considered, it is my conclusion that the death of Marilyn Monroe was caused by a self-administered overdose of sedative drugs and that the mode of death is probable suicide. The final toxicological report reveals that the barbiturate, previously reported as a lethal dose, has been positively identified as Nembutal by the toxicologist. In the course of completing his routine examination, the toxicologist Dr. Raymond Abernathy discovered in addition to the Nembutal present a large dose of chloral hydrate.

Following is the summary report by the Psychiatric Investigative Team, which has assisted me in collecting information in this case. This team was headed by Robert Litman, M.D., Norman Farberow, Ph. D., and Norman Tabachnick, M.D.:

Marilyn Monroe died on the night of August 4 or the early morning of August 5, 1962. Examination by the toxicology laboratory indicates that death was due to a self-administered overdose of sedative drugs. We have been asked, as consultants, to examine the life situation of the deceased and to give an opinion regarding the intent of Miss Monroe when she ingested the sedative drugs, which caused her death. From the data obtained, the following points are the most important and relevant:

Miss Monroe had suffered from psychiatric disturbance for a long time. She experienced severe fears and frequent depressions. Mood changes were abrupt and unpredictable. Among symptoms of disorganization, sleep disturbance was prominent, for which she had been taking sedative drugs for many rears. She was thus familiar with and experienced in the use of sedative drugs and well aware of their dangers.

Recently one of the main objectives of her psychiatric treatment had been the reduction of her intake drugs. This has been partially successful during the last two months. She was reported to be following doctor's orders in her use of the drugs; and the amount of drugs found in her home at the time of her death was not unusual.

In our investigation, we have learned that Miss Monroe had often expressed wishes to give up, to withdraw, and even to die. On more than one occasion in the past, when disappointed and depressed, she made a suicide attempt using sedative drugs. On those occasions, she had called for help and had been rescued.

From the information collected about the events of the evening of August 4th, it is our opinion that the same pattern was repeated except for the rescue. It has been our practice with similar information collected in other cases in the past to recommend a certification for such deaths as probable suicide.

Additional clues for suicide provided by the physical evidence are: (1) the high level of barbiturates and chloral hydrate in the blood which, with other evidence from the autopsy indicates the probable ingestion of a large amount of the drugs within a short period of time; (2) the completely empty bottle of Nembutal, the prescription for which was filled the day before the ingestion of the drugs; and (3) the locked door which was unusual.

On the basis of all the information obtained it is our opinion that the case is a probable suicide.

Apparently the Suicide Investigation Team had determined that Marilyn Monroe had suffered from depression and severe mood changes for many years. That, combined with an alleged history of substance abuse led them to believe she probably took her own life.

By law, these doctors were not required to reveal their sources of information, but according to their statement, most of their conclusions were based on psychological evaluations performed while Marilyn was still alive. There was only one person in Marilyn's life performing these types of evaluations, her psychiatrist, Dr. Ralph Greenson.

During the question and answer session, the same Associated Press reporter who spoke with Lester Goldberg, grilled Littman and Farberow about any evidence suggesting Marilyn Monroe could have been murdered. They were asked about rumors of Dr. Greenson recanting his statements regarding her being suicidal, and the presence of Robert Kennedy at her house the night she died. Both doctors calmly stated that, those aspects of the investigation were outside their mandate and referred those questions to Los Angeles Police Department officials.

Dr. Littman also discussed reading published news accounts about her life. One such report mentioned was Marilyn's alleged nervous breakdown during her filming of the "Misfits" in 1960. Monroe left the movie set for 10 days and supposedly checked herself into a hospital during that time. However, according to her diary, Marilyn was with John Kennedy at a Beverly Hills Fundraiser for his election campaign, and she described the nervous breakdown as an excuse for a weeklong fling.

The Suicide Investigation Team also claimed they uncovered evidence showing Marilyn had tried to take her own life several times before. This information must also have been acquired from tabloid newspaper accounts. During my subsequent investigation of her case, I spoke with many of Marilyn's friends and none of her close acquaintances remembered when any actual suicide attempts ever occurred.

Dr. Littman and Dr. Farberow's report seemed to indicate that the Los Angeles Police Department had also guided and influenced their decision. That meant either they or Dr. Curphey had talked to police officials. After the press conference, I went to Dr. Curphey to obtain all data from the Suicide Team 's investigation for Marilyn's private folder, and the people they interviewed for Marilyn's folder. Curphey informed me that these reports were all oral and there are no written records available.

Let me say now, because I was there, that no thorough investigation was ever performed by the Suicide Team. They provided me with a list of people they wanted to speak to, but only three witnesses were set up for interviews: Dr. Engelberg, Dr. Greenson, and Marilyn's publicist Pat Newcomb. I never could verify they spoke with these three, but no official record of any interviews exists. I even checked with the medical and investigative stenographers to ask if any notes were submitted to them for typing and they all said no.

The police reports on the other hand, were public record and copies accompanied each public file as a matter of course. A follow up report from the Los Angeles Police Department was never sent, or else Dr. Curphey must have personally received them. Either way, according to county ordinances, you couldn't close a case without these documents. I even asked Curphey if the Suicide team had received a police report, but he said none of their information was available. Apparently, it was just a doctor's thing where they all sat around with Engelberg and Greenson to discuss and determine how she died.

In the days that followed, while gathering my files, all the original paperwork began to disappear. For instance, the original toxicology report that had shown no poison in the blood now revealed a high concentration of barbiturates in the liver. The new dosage in her blood, which was determined before microscopic test had returned, was enough to have killed her 10 times over. The physical diagram that had shown the bruises on the body was gone and replaced by one that showed no marks. The original toxicology report was missing and the police statement to our first call deputy was gone. Even the property log came up missing.

A few days later, while sitting at my desk, I was approached by a man claiming to be a forensics investigator from the office. I wasn't sure if I had seen him around before, but he said he needed to discuss some official business and asked could we meet for lunch. He seemed to know me on a first name basis, but to this day I am unable to recall his.

At lunch, he said that the higher ups were concerned about my misgivings in regards to the Monroe case. He asked me if I thought Marilyn was murdered. I told him there wasn't enough evidence to support murder, but more than likely she didn't commit suicide.

The man asked if I knew what happened to her property. I told him it was taken out of the safe, without being signed for and by someone with a key. His reaction seemed to suggest he thought I knew more, or perhaps even had it myself, but he didn't ask anything else about it. We ate lunch and talked for nearly an hour about the case and people at the office, including Dr. Curphey. He knew everybody by name and appeared to be genuinely concerned about me.

During our conversation he steadily emphasized how important it was for us to be teammates and look out for each other. He said,

"Lionel, we all know you're a hard working family man with 3 kids and we're going to look out for you. As we were leaving, he handed me a credit card and told me, "this is to help you and the family get a little further ahead. Buy some things you need and I'll get the card later."

It seemed a little odd, but for a young 22-year old man, and sole supporter of his family, all I could think was why not? Especially after that long pep talk about looking out for each other and being teammates. After finishing my shift, I went to a local tire store and purchased new tires for my car, which were worn out from my daily ride downtown.

When I arrived back at work the next day, Dr. Curphey had announced that he or his Administrative Assistant would be answering all inquiries about the Monroe case. They revealed to the press that the overdose had been self-administered and the pills were swallowed in one gulp. Needless to say, this was now the official statement and released to almost every news agency in the world.

I had read Dr. Noguchi's preliminary autopsy report, and he never concluded how these barbiturates were introduced to the body. There was never any official statement of those facts or any mention of the 30 pills that Dr. Noguchi found lodged in her throat. There was no trace of any other prescription drugs she was known to be taking.

There were plenty of phone calls from her friends and fans, who thought the suicide finding was a slur on Marilyn's character and were demanding that the Coroner convene an Inquest into her death. Others, including the media, suspected someone else had administered the overdose, perhaps by injection or suppository.

Most disturbing was the fate of specimens taken from Monroe's body during the autopsy. When Dr. Noguchi asked the lab to test Marilyn's tissue samples again, he was told they had already been destroyed on orders from Dr. Curphey.

As far as the Coroner was concerned, the investigation into the death of Marilyn Monroe had come to an end. The case was put on my desk with instructions to close as soon as possible. The death certificate inside the file gave the cause of death as acute barbiturate poisoning due to ingestion of overdose. In the space for Mode of Death, autopsy surgeon Dr. Thomas Noguchi circled Suicide adding the word probable.

It was normal procedure that the Deputy who handles the investigation signs the death certificate on behave of the Coroner. His signature certifies that all laws had been complied with for the State of California. I went to see Dr. Curphey to get the necessary information to close the file, but he told me he was not ready to release the information and to sign it with what I have.

When asked about the inaccurate information that was

in the file, Curphey went into a rage and said,

"Grandison you are in over your head. I warned you about this. Sign it or else."

This was another incident of pressure from him to circumvent county policy. Normally Curphey would have been adamant about following county rules and regulations, but it was apparent that Marilyn Monroe's case was anything but normal. He then handed me a press release stating:

PRESS RELEASE

There was no credible evidence supporting a murder theory. There was a possibility that the death had been accidental, but suicide was more likely.

Theodore Curphey, Coroner of Los Angeles County

He said give all the Deputies this release and regard it as the official statement. I remember walking down the hall saying to myself, "What business is this of mine? He's the boss and if this is the way it's supposed to go, than so be it." He must have known something that wasn't part of the file. I thought maybe it's time for me to be a team player. So, reluctantly, I signed the death certificate, and hoped to never hear the name Marilyn Monroe again.

Driving home, I remember having a bad taste in my mouth. Team player or not, everything about that Marilyn Monroe case was wrong, and now I was part of the cover-up. A few months earlier, I had seen another instance of the Coroner's abuse of power. In April, LAPD had shot an unarmed Black Muslim at his house of worship. The Mayor of Los Angeles, Sam Yorty, had come out and arduously stated to not look at this "militant group" as having a house of worship.

He went on to say that the police had reason to believe that guns were at the location, and plots to undermine the government existed within this group. Of course, there were neither guns nor plots, just an innocent dead citizen and a lot of wounded people.

Previously, my only interaction with Muslims had been with their newspaper, Muhammad Speaks. I would buy it from time to time and read what they were saying about the African American heritage. They were an aggressive group on the streets of Los Angeles, promoting a change for America in their treatment of African Americans. The Nation of Islam was part of the new revolutionary movement, which included the Black Panthers, Southern Christian Leadership Conference, and others who were pushing their idea of Freedom, Justice, and Equality.

I had never considered myself a part of these movements, but certain events, such as the lynching of 14-year-old Emmitt Till in Mississippi, made me wonder about the future of African Americans. In the case of Emmitt Till, the group of Ku Klux Klan members who ruthlessly battered and hung this teenager were found innocent of all charges.

California was not a place where they had segregated facilities, and the courts ostensibly followed the law in dealing with African Americans. Most of the people who lived here were civilized and could see the bright future of an integrated America, but racism was still present, particularly in law enforcement and employment.

An inquest was scheduled to determine if anyone was criminally responsible for the death of Ronald Stokes, an African-American killed in South Central Los Angeles. The Inquest deputy was Charles Langhauser, who controlled the proceedings on behalf of the Coroner.

LAPD provided all the witnesses, and no private citizens were allowed to testify. Normal procedure was to have the City, District Attorney, or outside counsels, submit questions that Langhauser would ask under oath to any witnesses called. He alone had subpoena powers.

It was my case and I received a call from the Stokes family attorney, regarding the inquest. He was asking about the procedure for submitting questions to the police officers. Giving the call to the Inquest Deputy, who was standing at my desk, I heard him tell the attorney,

"Just bring your questions to the Inquest, and there would be no problem."

Having worked a number of Inquests, I knew that all questions must be submitted to the Inquest deputy seventy-two hours in advance.

On the day of the Inquest, the press pool heard there would be an appearance from Malcolm X, the proclaimed Black Militant. Malcolm embodied the struggle for equal justice under the law, which was essentially the same cry of the Civil Rights Movement under Dr. Martin Luther King.

The Washington Post and the New York Times had covered Malcolm X's accusation of the New York Police Department mishandling African American prisoners while in their custody. This was his first major incident on the West Coast.

He was speaking to groups all around the city and leading an effort to prosecute the officers involved in the shooting. When Malcolm X walked into the Coroner's Office, a hush came over room. There were four well-groomed men with him, who were also Muslims, standing at attention near the counter. The family's lawyer, whose name was Charles Brody, walked in with them.

Brody was one of the top black legal minds in Los Angeles. His resume was extensive, and he was also the first to hire a young Johnny Cochran. He leaned on the counter and asked the clerk where to deliver his questions. Armand then called the supervising deputy, who explained that no questions could be posed because they were not submitted in time. The hall was full of newspapermen and Inquest witnesses, mostly Los Angeles Police Officers, listening carefully to what was happening.

Malcolm cried cover-up and a brief scuffle occurred. To avoid calling Sheriff Deputies, I pulled the Nation of Islam members aside and told Malcolm to give me five questions, which I then placed under the papers that Inquest Deputy

Langhauser had on the bench. Although only one of them was asked at the Inquest, there was no doubt who was responsible for putting that question there.

The shooting was found to be justifiable and no one was criminally responsible. Needless to say, this meant another trip to Curphey's office, but established ties with the Muslim

community that would play a huge part in my future. They were very appreciative for my efforts to give them a voice in the proceeding.

It's important to understand that every case was significant to me. My feelings were that government offices should be colorblind and administer the law equally. I handled all kinds of cases including sudden deaths for no apparent reason, tragic accidents where identification was in question, homicides where life was ended in a cruel manner, and both questionable and unquestionable suicides.

In most cases, the next of kin was devastated and these were highly emotional times for the families. I signed temporary death certificates to get their love ones buried, helped with legal matters such as insurance and estates, and also mediated next of kin problems that the investigating Deputy had to resolve. People that came into our office found a friend that would use the power of the Coroner's Office to protect their rights, when dealing with government agencies

CHAPTER 6:
After The Coroner's Office

Despite still struggling with having signed the death certificate, it was business as usual at the Coroner's office. There was never a shortage of work. However, things did seem a little less hectic with the stress of Marilyn's case behind me. That was very short lived.

Days after closing the case, I arrived to work and was confronted by investigators from the District Attorneys office, who wanted to ask me some questions about a missing credit card. As it turned out, the card given to me by that man during lunch had come from the property of a closed Coroner's case. That credit card was still sitting at my desk waiting to be picked up. When I bought the tires using the credit card, it just didn't feel right and I never used it again. After telling the investigators what happened and where the card was, I was arrested and taken to jail.

During my interrogation, an endless stream of police and law officials questioned me, but I never knew who anybody was. I tried to explain what happened, but my story must have seemed was absolutely ridiculous. A guy, who said he was from the office, gave me the card and said get myself some things? Even I had a hard time believing that story, even when it had happened to me.

For years, I believed that Dr. Curphey had sent this man to set me up. Later, the possibility of a larger conspiracy to discredit me became all too apparent. Marilyn's diary

contained highly sensitive information about United States Government agencies, and that book had been in my possession. Either way, it really didn't matter. I had got caught in a huge bear trap, and there was no getting out.

The District Attorney asked me why someone would set me up like that. At the time, I really wasn't sure why this had happened, but what first came to mind was the Marilyn Monroe case and her diary. Lester Goldberg had told me this was a hot potato and some heavy hitters were involved, but I never thought it could come to this.

There was no choice but to tell District Attorney investigators everything about the case and the existence of her diary. I described what she wrote about, including working for the FBI and her relationship with the Kennedy's. I explained how poorly her death investigation was handled and how Dr. Curphey forced me to sign her death certificate.

After hours of interrogation, I was told not to mention this to anybody or talk about the man who originally stole the credit card. They said if I complied with these terms a, lenient verdict would be given. My attorney was livid when he discovered how candid my answers were in lieu of the fact the District Attorney was not attempting to find the guy who had given me the stolen property. However, I didn't believe there was anything to hide. Unfortunately, in the end, I became the perfect fall guy.

The court ruled I hadn't stolen the card nor forged the name, but was guilty of receiving stolen property and granted probation as my lenient sentence. The news media had a field day on the story. Embarrassed and labeled a criminal, I resigned from the Coroner's Office in disgrace.

As the dust began to settle, my next step was simply trying to get on with my life. With no income to pay the monthly rent and food bills, times quickly became difficult for our family. The prospects for employment were very slim because of my record and notoriety. After much soul searching, I decided to enroll at Los Angeles City College, and pursue a career in communications.

The world of television and radio had fascinated me since being a young child. At 9 years old, I appeared on several episodes of the Art Linkletter "People Are Funny" television show. That experience captivated my imagination and influenced my interest in communications. I was fortunate to have a family that provided their full support. With me now taking classes, my wife began working for the first time, while my Grandmother helped with the kids.

Just more than a year later, I was stunned by the announcement that President John F. Kennedy had been assassinated. As I sat there watching the news report, all I could think about was Marilyn's diary. Could there have been a connection between what I had read and the President's death? To tell the truth, I had a surreal feeling about the whole thing. It was like deja vu. The only good thing was that I wasn't involved. Or was I?

As new information would begin to surface, I began to think the latter. Two days after Kennedy's death, a man killed his accused assassin, Lee Harvey Oswald, at Dallas Police Headquarters. That man, Jack Ruby, had extensive ties with Sam Giancana and the mafia.

The President's Commission on the Assassination of President Kennedy, better known as the Warren Commission, was established in the days following the Kennedy assassination. Reports began to surface that Lee Harvey Oswald had close ties to Cuba and the CIA.

Marilyn had written about the obsession President Kennedy and the CIA had with killing Castro. They were so desperate to kill him, that their plot included using Mafia gangsters.

The Warren Commission investigation uncovered some startling facts. Apparently, the Russians and Cubans had considered Oswald a Federal Agent. The KGB suspected him of being a false defector, sent to Russia to spy for the United States. Castro claimed that when Oswald left Russia he went to Mexico in search of information on the missile bases being constructed off the coast of the United States.

Information about Oswald's stay in Mexico City, prior to the assassination of JFK, was reported in a Classified Top Secret Document. After receiving the report, the Warren Commission acknowledged the existence of CIA surveillance photos showing Oswald entering Fair Play For Cuba meetings in Mexico.

The disposition of these photographs and who else was in the said photos was not disclosed. There was no doubt he was in Mexico in February 1962. This would leave a strong possibility of him being there the same time as Marilyn. If I was to believe the Cuban scenario with the CIA and Mafia, or the other pages that were in her book, then it was not far fetched to assume there could be an Oswald-Marilyn connection.

These were the first pieces of a complex puzzle that began to come together. Although I was an outsider looking in now, it was plain to see the same group of agencies was involved. There were still many more puzzle pieces and unanswered questions. However, there were two things looming large in my mind. Who introduced Marilyn Monroe to John F. Kennedy, and why?

I went to work for a record distributor that marketed releases by Cameo Parkway artists Bobby Rydell and Chubby Checker. They were two of the biggest artists of the times. Just to show you the coincidence that has followed me, the first promotional campaign assigned to me, where my decisions really mattered, was a novelty remake of "Wild Thing" by an impressionist imitating Robert F. Kennedy under the name Senator Bobby. How dare this set of characters follow me into my private life.

Unfortunately, the death of John Kennedy brought back

memories of Marilyn's case to someone other than me. It had been a very difficult time following my experience at the Coroner's Office, extremely tough on me and my wife. One evening, a few weeks following the assassination, she said,

"This whole situation is your fault. I told you to put that damn diary down and act like you never saw it. If you would have just did that and minded your own business, none of this would have ever happened."

The pressure had finally gottten too much for both of us and we agreed to separate and ultimately were divorced.

The time following my divorce was a very strenous period of my life. Fortunately, I was still close to my kids, who were regular visitors at my Grandmother's house. My mother had moved in and was also babysitting. The love these two women provided during this time allowed me and my ex-wife to pursue our lives, knowing our children always had someone willing and wanting to care for them.

During the mid-sixties, racial tensions in Los Angeles were at an all time high. Black power movements such as the Nation of Islam, Black Panther Party, Student Non-Violent Coordinating Committee (SNCC), and other activist were confronting numerous issues facing the African-American community. Segregation, police brutality, and racism was something every black person in America had to deal with and I was no different.

On February 25, 1965 the news that Malcolm X was killed stimulated something inside of me like never before.

From the time we met in 1962 at the Coroner's office, and even before then, Malcolm represented the fighting spirit of all Americans who truly believed in the concept of freedom, justice, and equality. Rumors were floating around the black community, saying that the FBI was involved in Malcolm's death. When I thought about how the Federal Bureau of Investigation had used Marilyn Monroe back in the 1950's, it wasn't surprising at all to hear of their involvment. The rumors claimed that agents from the FBI had infiltrated the Nation of Islam and instigated the in-fighting between Malcolm and their leader, the Honorable Elijan Muhammad.

Years later, I would discover that both the CIA and FBI were making plans to assassinate Malcolm. A couple of names from the past came up, Robert Maheu and Johnny Roselli, both of whom were contracted to kill Malcolm, according to FBI disclosures. Marilyn wrote extensivley about Maheu and Roselli in her diary and these two figures were still wreaking havoc in other peoples lives. Another question also came to mind, did either of them have anything to do with Kennedy's assassination?

I was awakened on August 12, 1965 by a phone call from one of my associates Earl Anthony, a law student from USC and Minister of Information for the Black Panther Party. He said a California highway patrolman had arrested a whole family in Watts and roughed up the mother as a crowd of a couple hundred people gathered around the scene.

That afternoon, a community meeting was scheduled, which Earl wanted me to attend. The purpose was to discuss solutions to the problems concerning public unrest in South Central Los Angeles. This was little out of my area of expertise, but my friend felt there needed to be some young people at the meeting. As I drove through the city, large crowds of people were gathered in the streets, throwing objects at cars including police patrol ones.

The number one issue at the meeting was the accepted policy of police brutality by the Los Angeles Police Department. The issues of jobs and discrimination by the business community were a close second. At the meeting, about two hundred people were gathered, including preachers, church members, some business owners, a representative from the local Black bank, and a number of young African Americans, who were frustrated by the lack of employment opportunities. Labor unions were making their push with strikes across the country, and African Americans were making their stand against exclusion.

Low paying Civil Service jobs made up the bulk of workers in the African American community. Most of the income that was derived came from Los Angeles City or County employment, because it was steady work. At that time major corporations only hired 5% minority employees and even that was divided up between Latinos and Blacks.

The outcry that emerged against racism and discrimination exploded like a timebomb. Black leaders pleaded to restore order in the community, but it was too late. When I drove home, I heard a rallying cry from a local radio personality named Magnificent Montague, "burn, baby, burn". He was fond of yelling "Burn" when he played a hit record. When his listeners called him on the air, they followed suit. But this was no time for comedy, and the phrase set the tone for what was to come.

The Watts Riots began that night. By the time the second community meeting was convened, over 3,000 national guardsmen had joined the police, trying to maintain order on the streets. Jeeploads of heavily armed soldiers were prowling the neighborhoods and randomly shooting.

Inside a run-down, two-story building, across the street from Green Meadows Park in Los Angeles, several hundred angry citizens stated they didn't feel bad about what was happening. The general consensus was the time had come to make our feelings known and police brutality was a good place to start.

"Burn, baby, burn," someone yelled, to a chorus of thundering applause.

I understood the anger and resentment the community was feeling towards the establishment. My life experiences had made me very sympathetic towards this type of violent reaction. However, I wasn't sure if this was the answer.

I once heard Malcolm X say how to avoid this type of civil disturbance.

"Step Up and Do For Self. We're paying taxes and those tax dollars are what allows the police to beat us up. We have to develop our own economy to strengthen the black community."

Those remarks reflected my feelings towards our situation and they needed to echo through out South Central Los Angeles.

There was a curfew on, and the police were stopping cars to search for weapons. Officers were roughing up everybody, especially teenagers gathered in the streets. Leaving the meeting, I noticed members of the Black Muslim security team from Temple number 27 in Los Angeles, helping people who attended the meeting return safely to their cars and homes. One of them was Captain Edward Rasheed, who Malcolm X had introduced me to in 1962 at the Coroner's office incident.

Observing his professionalism and dedication to the community made me realize that every African-American had an obligation to their people. If rioting is not the answer then we owe it to ourselves to discover what is. When the smoke cleared from the Watts Riots of 1965, 34 people had been killed, over one thousand injured and over thirty-five hundred American citizens arrested.

Marilyn's old friend, J. Edgar Hoover, believed that the riots were linked to Communist groups, who blamed unemployment and prejudice as the cause. LAPD Chief William Parker also fueled the tension by publicly labeling the people he saw involved in the riots as "monkeys in the zoo." In the end, one eye-catching fact was that before the Watts Riots, 69% of the Black community lived below the poverty level. This decreased to 39% in the years following, indicating the Black community's growth was alive and prospering.

In 1961, when Robert Kennedy headed the Justice Department, he promoted racial diversity in the formally all white Justice Department and appointed the largest number of African Americans to serve in any federal department up to that time. Kennedy strengthened the Civil Rights Division and stringently enforced laws protecting workers' right to organize trade unions and formally strike against employers.

He also began planning for a program called the 'War on Poverty." Marilyn and Bobby Kennedy were having their affair during that time, and she described her meetings at the so-called Western White House with Kennedy and the other planners to one of her close friends. I did not read this in the diary, but during my conversation with her friend, Jeanne Carmen, she tried to put into context what Marilyn had said.

Marilyn told her, she convinced the War on Poverty planners that what was really needed was a new citizen's movement whose strength rested in grassroots community action. Carmine was astonished that Marilyn even knew anything about instruments for social change, but said Marilyn was very proud of herself.

The apparent result of these sessions was President

Lyndon Johnson's War on Poverty. The strategy had begun in the Kennedy administration and provided Johnson with a format for the program. The Office of Economic Opportunity was fully committed to this grass roots strategy that Marilyn had apparently suggested.

I had the opportunity to join this War on Poverty by attending classes at San Diego State University and the University of California, Berkeley. The Federal Government was recruiting candidates to operate their proposed manpower training programs. They were interviewing and testing throughout the country to get potential counselors and instructors to educate and prepare disadvantaged youth for the job market. The classes were held on at least six major university campuses and offered Masters Program credits for attending.

This brought together a highly motivated group of individuals who saw their role in society as preparing the minority community for its entrance into the majority culture. A small percentage of African Americans and Latinos were admitted to this exclusive group, and the administration soon realized how critical their perspective was for communicating with the minorities they were trying to train.

The Johnson Administration began to implement community action programs. These would provide training and jobs for young men and women coming from impoverished families and neighborhoods. They offered me a job as an employment specialist in this noble effort. The only problem was after we trained the disadvantaged youth, there were no jobs for them.

Disappointed with the program, I left Northern California and returned to Los Angeles just in time for the most unbelievable story of the year. Senator Robert Kennedy had been assassinated. He was shot and killed in front of 50 or 60 eyewitnesses at the Coconut Grove Hotel in Los Angeles.

This Marilyn saga just refused to die. Now, all three of them were dead and it was mind-bending. What were the odds of them all dying within less than six years of each other? They had to be astronomical. According to what I read in the diary, the relationship these three shared was extensive and intricate. This couldn't be a coincidence.

Both Kennedys were dead. Moreover, they had been brutally murdered. What did it all mean? During the past few years, I had been following how the JFK murder was quickly coming apart. New revelations had begun to surface about the CIA being involved and accounts of multiple shooters.

There were 4 or 5 different accounts of Robert Kennedy's assassination. The person arrested, Sirhan Sirhan, was deemed as psychotic by even prosecution psychiatrists and unfit to stand trial. But the judge disagreed and Sirhan was made to stand trial anyway. He would later claim he had been hypnotized or brainwashed. Sirhan was convicted and sentenced to death for assassinating Kennedy. That conviction was later commuted to a life sentence.

My old friend, Dr. Thomas Noguchi, performed the Autopsy. He said in the autopsy report that three bullets had hit Kennedy. A fourth damaged his suit coat and came upward at about an 80-degree angle. Noguchi and LAPD criminologist DeWayne Wolfer both conducted powder tests and concluded that the three body shots came from about an inch away.

Later, Noguchi pointed out that he had refrained from saying whether there could have been a second shooter. The LAPD destroyed a large amount of evidence, and what survived from the police file was not released until twenty years later. What else was new?

This was a jigsaw puzzle of epic proportions. Two members of America's best-known family were dead and one of Hollywood's best-known actresses was dead. What did they all have in common? Marilyn's little red book. That was too much drama for me. I shook my head and said,

"This chapter of my life is now finally closed."

CHAPTER 7:
Marilyn Calls Out

In 1974, I was producing a Public Affairs radio series for Capital Cities Communications in Los Angeles. Cap Cities, as they came to be known, was a very progressive station group, who embraced Federal Communications Commission rules to provide programming for minority communities. In their major markets, WJR-AM-FM in Detroit and KPOL AM-FM in Los Angeles, they began broadcasting intelligent Public Affairs programs for Latino and African American audiences.

My organization, Project BAIT was the producer of one of these shows. Spearheaded by Dave Rambo in Detroit, and my mentor Jim Crossen in Los Angeles, we were among the first to take advantage of these new FCC rules. We began airing a weekly show called "Who Cares," which became extremely popular and gave me the opportunity to meet various interesting people from many walks of life.

By chance, one of our producers scheduled an interview with an author who had written a book called "The Life and Curious Death of Marilyn Monroe." Now you can imagine my thoughts when that press release came to me. Twelve years after my hectic experience, Marilyn seemed to be calling out again.

The author's name was Robert Slatzer. I didn't know what to expect when he came into the studio. Slatzer's bio said he was the central voice that proclaimed Marilyn's death was not suicide. While our producer was interviewing him, I glanced through the pages of his book. His research was incredible. As I thumbed through, there was even a chapter that discussed the autopsy and the Coroner's handling of the evidence.

Although he didn't have all the information right, he did have copies of original files from the case and numerous photos, including the crime scene. These were things I hadn't seen in more than a decade. As I was looking through the documents in his book, low and behold there was a copy of her death certificate with my signature on it.

Listening to the interview, Slatzer was convinced that Marilyn had been murdered and there was a conspiracy to cover it up because of a Kennedy connection. He said his interest was stimulated by the fact that he was once married to Marilyn, and Fox Studios had it annulled. I didn't know what to think about him, but the things he was saying began filling in some blanks like never before.

He told us a story about wire tapers who had bugged Marilyn's house. Bernard Spindel, an expert in audio surveillance, and his partner Fred Otash were hired by Teamster Union Boss Jimmy Hoffa to bug Marilyn's residence. Slatzer had uncovered massive details about these wire tapers and heard some of their recordings.

Slatzer said he discovered that Hoffa wanted to locate a diary that Marilyn had boasted was in her possession. The wire tapers claimed the union boss was desperately trying to blackmail Attorney General, Bobby Kennedy, and make him drop the racketeering charges he was pursuing. Slatzer was also told that three members of the Giancana family in Chicago were sent to keep an eye on the wiretap.

Mafia boss, Sam Giancana, knew that Marilyn had knowledge of his participation in the CIA plot to kill Castro. She had been present when he and Johnny Roselli agreed to participate in the plot with President Kennedy and CIA operatives. The wire tapers said Giancana heard Marilyn tell some people about a press conference and her plans to, "Tell it All." They told Slatzer she had made these comments at a Frank Sinatra party in Lake Tahoe the weekend before she died.

Talk about a bombshell. Marilyn had written about that party in her diary and many other things, Robert Slatzer was corroborating. I was completely stunned by what he was saying. How could this have happened? A man once married to Marilyn Monroe coming into the studio and confirming things I read in her diary. Yes indeed, Marilyn was calling out.

When Slatzer finished the interview, I introduced myself and informed him of my connection to the case. The look on his face was priceless. Needless to say, he was extremely surprised and had tons of questions for me. We reminisced a few moments, and then he asked if I would be interested in coming to his office for further discussion.

It was hard to comprehend how this Marilyn Monroe case kept coming back for more. No matter where I was or what I did, it had an uncanny ability to find me. Whatever my destiny was with this case, it was time to see it through. Deep in my heart, I always knew something was wrong, and if Marilyn was really murdered, could that be simply ignored? I agreed to meet with him and discuss my official Coroner's investigation.

Slatzer had an office at the old Taft Building on Hollywood Boulevard and Vine. Walking up to the building entrance, I was still somewhat apprehensive about getting involved with this case again. The night before, I pulled out my old notes and refreshed my memory about the things that had happened at the Coroner's Office. It brought back deep-rooted feelings from that period of my life, and they all weren't good. Still this was something that had to be done. The time had come to talk about my experiences.

Slatzer, who told me to call him Bob, was the kind of man who could immediately put you at ease. He was very personable, with a great sense of humor and strong character to match. Bob repeated his incredible story of having been married to Marilyn Monroe. He said they loved each other as deep as anyone could love and were wed in Mexico. When the studio discovered what had happened, they had made Marilyn get an annulment.

There was no doubt Bob still loved Marilyn. He showed me pictures of them, happy and together, and explained how he was dedicated to exposing the cover up around her death. For him, there was absolutely no doubt in his mind that Marilyn was murdered.

He began to explain more of the evidence he had uncovered during his years of investigation. Much of it was centered on the cover-up at the house that night. Bob showed me a picture of the window that Dr. Greenson had allegedly broke to enter Marilyn's room, after seeing her lying motionless on the bed. But the broken glass was on the outside. Bob claimed the window had been broken from the inside of the house.

I described to him my experiences at the Coroner's office the morning she died, including how the studio attempted to remove her body from the crime scene. I told my story of how Dr. Curphey mishandled the case, forced me to sign the death certificate, and how I had been set-up by that infamous mysterious stranger.

It didn't take long for our conversation to turn towards the Kennedy's. He began to say specific things about Bobby Kennedy that were referenced in Marilyn's diary passages. That's when I decided to tell him there had been a journal in her property that detailed her encounter with both Kennedy's, supporting many things he was saying in his book.

Bob looked at me for a moment with those eyes of his and only said,

"Describe it to me."

I told him my remembrance of the diary's appearance, and he said he had seen it before. Bob informed me that Marilyn had shared the diary with him a few weeks before she died. In his new book, he wrote about some of the passages he read.

Bob asked if I knew what happened to the diary and I told him all of Marilyn's property had disappeared from the Coroner's Office, but my belief was that Dr. Curphey had taken it. He claimed there were also two other people who knew what was in the diary, Jeannie Carmine and Terry Moore. I remembered that Marilyn had mentioned them frequently in her writings.

Bob said it was common knowledge that she would write things down and that it was his belief the contents of her diary were what got her murdered. He said the wire tapers stated their surveillance equipment was not the only devices at the house, there were at least 2 others recording units they identified as government property. This meant the FBI and CIA were keeping tabs on Marilyn's exploits as well.

It felt uncomfortable, hearing that Marilyn possibly was

killed because of what was in the diary. In 1962, the District Attorney had warned me not to go into details about the Marilyn Monroe case, so I had never discussed the information with anyone.

Bob wanted me to go public with what I knew. He said with my support as an ex-county official, we could get the Los Angeles County Board of Supervisors to reopen the case. Could you imagine me inviting the FBI, the Kennedy family, the District Attorney, the Mafia, and the CIA back into my life to create havoc again?

At this point, there really wasn't much choice. I told Bob he would have my support and that I was willing to testifying how the Coroner's Office mishandled the investigation. However, Bob was also informed that the contents of the diary where something that could not be discussed.

"What I read in the diary must remain confidential," I told him. He agreed, paused for a moment then playfully said,

"So what did you read?" We both laughed.

If I carried on with this, my destiny with Marilyn Monroe would be cemented and turning back would no longer be an option. We began to retrace what we knew about her case, and Bob revealed additional information about the wire tapers he discussed during the radio interview.

Bob told me he heard audiotapes of what happened at Marilyn's house the final two days of her life. Most of what he listened to involved Robert Kennedy, these conversations occurring on Friday, August 3, and Saturday, August 4, of 1962.

Bob said Marilyn's exchanges with Bobby Kennedy were very heated over those final days. There was a huge phone argument, and on the tape, Marilyn was heard answering a call from Bobby Kennedy, who told her he was coming over that evening but never showed up.

The highlight of these audiotapes was Bobby Kennedy's two visits to Marilyn's house. In a state of rage, Bob heard him saying,

"I was a fool, taking you to those meetings. Where in the hell is that damn diary."

Bob said Marilyn responded with,

"The diary is mine. You weren't the first to take me to some damn meetings, but come to the press conference, you'll get a good look for yourself."

Bob said he could hear Kennedy leaving and then Marilyn made some phone calls, having conversations with Dr. Greenson and Jeanne Carmine.

Bob said Kennedy returned later with Peter Lawford, and he could hear someone throwing things and slamming drawers. He heard yelling from who he believed was Bobby Kennedy, saying,

"Where's that damn book, Marilyn?"

Then he described hearing a loud noise and scream that seemed to be Marilyn falling, and could also hear her crying.

I told Bob that Marilyn had written about all those incidents in her diary.

Recalling what she wrote,

"They want me to call off the press conference. Too late."

"Bobby was really mad. Acted crazy and searched all my stuff. Told him it's mine. I'll never let him have it."

"Bobby came back with Peter. Shook me until I was dizzy and threw me on the bed. Should call the doctor..."

I always believed that Marilyn had made these final entries the night she died. I also told Bob about the press release that had arrived with the rest of her personal property. He said Marilyn had told him about the press conference and her plans to "blow the lid off the whole damned thing." Bob believed all of this was about Robert Kennedy, but I hadn't shared with him the depth of her involvement with the Government's Intelligence Agencies.

Bob said that while listening to that part of the tape, the wire taper told him he overheard one of the Chicago guys saying,

"We could kill her tonight and blame it on that rich boy Kennedy."

As the tape kept playing, he heard Kennedy leave the house once again. Bob said Marilyn then made several more phone calls, including another to Dr. Greenson, asking him if he removed her bottle of Nembutal when he was there earlier. Greenson told her no. The tape ended after that.

The wire tapers claimed the Chicago gangsters left soon thereafter. They told Slatzer it was never their plan to have that type of involvement. Wiretapping was one thing, but murder was another. He said they wouldn't discuss what was recorded next. Bob recounted listening to about 3 or 4 hours of these tapes, and walked away believing he had not heard everything.

He said what was on the tapes didn't sound staged, it seemed very authentic and was believable. The real test of credibility for these tapes was the voices. Bob related that he was sure it was Marilyn's voice, and Kennedy's Boston accent was easy to recognize.

I asked Bob what happened to the audiotapes of Marilyn's last night alive and he told me a New York prosecutor had confiscated Spindel's original copy as evidence. When he requested their return, they told him the tapes were lost. Why wasn't I surprised about a piece of critical evidence disappearing? Shortly thereafter, Bernard Spindel mysteriously died in a prison jail cell. The FBI had already taken his partner, Fred Otash's, copy in 1963, following President Kennedy's assassination.

"Lionel, I've never believed in fate, but I do believe it was our destiny meet. We're going to let the world know what really happened to Marilyn." Bob said at the conclusion of our meeting. His passion was overwhelming.

Incredibly, a few months later, Jimmy Hoffa disappeared, never to be heard from again. One thing Bob and I had both seen in Marilyn's diary was her references to Hoffa.

Marilyn had written,

I met Jimmy Hoffa at Frank's party... Sam and him were asking about Bobby...

"Bobby was on the phone most of the night... It was something about putting that guy Hoffa in jail..."

Bob said he read some of those same passages and had also wrote about them in his book. He said Marilyn never fully understood who Jimmy Hoffa was and what he was involved in. In his opinion, Bobby Kennedy had put her in the middle of a crossfire that existed between Hoffa, Sam Giancana and himself.

When the radio show featuring his interview aired, it was an enormous success. Inquiries came in from stations around the country, wanting to air the Marilyn Monroe program. We decided to produce a follow-up show, centering on Hoffa's involvement with Marilyn. We wanted to talk about the Teamsters leader's close ties to Organized Crime and how that impacted her death.

We began to schedule people to appear on the show, but soon discovered there weren't many takers. The Hoffa era had made a tremendous social impact. Most people only wanted to discuss the good things Hoffa had done. We were fortunate to interview the President of Western Carloading, a trucking firm in Los Angeles, who told us a story about Hoffa using the Mafia to intimidate strike busters and non-union workers.

The only other people who would talk about Hoffa's ties to the Mafia were a couple of representatives from the Teamsters union. One union representative told us that Jimmy Hoffa's career literally touched millions of workers in this country. The International Brotherhood of Teamsters organized truck drivers and warehousemen nationwide. As the unions began to expand, they negotiated agreements, to cover all employers in a given industry. This paved the way for wages that would give the workers a comfortable middle class lifestyle. With this came a political power that started to manifest itself in the mid fifties.

Hoffa played a major role in the union's skillful use of worker strikes, which eventually brought them to a position of being one of the most powerful movements in the United States. The picket lines were a microcosm of America with Latinos, Asians, European immigrants, African Americans, and Whites standing shoulder to shoulder for fair wages.

They didn't have to like or trust each other, but they understood the need to support each other.

The Union Rep went on to say that J. Edgar Hoover took the confrontations to a higher level by accusing the strikers of being socialist whenever commerce came to a standstill. Hoover claimed that unions and integration posed the biggest threats to America moving forward. However, there was little public support for the FBI or the multi national corporations.

This shift in public opinion was probably due to the growing evidence of Hoover's past willingness to focus huge resources to undermine the reputation of his targets. Many more people were now aware of how the FBI gathered personal information on American citizens. They had become known for trying to destroy people like Dr. Martin Luther King and organizations such as Teamsters Union.

Another union member stated that when Hoffa accused Congress of passing strike breaking, union-busting Bills, Senator John Kennedy responded with a full scale U.S. Government criminal investigation of the Teamster's Union. The United States Senate established the Select Committee on Improper Activities in Labor and Management, giving them broad subpoena and investigative powers. They hired a young Robert Kennedy as the subcommittee's chief counsel and investigator. This was his first national exposure.

A strange and contentious relationship developed between Bobby Kennedy and Hoffa that would last the rest of their lives. During the show, we included the sound track from Kennedy's intense questioning of Hoffa at the Senate hearings, which initiated the hatred between the two men. Marilyn witnessed firsthand the Hoffa-Robert Kennedy dispute.

A few old-timers we talked to gave some insights into why they thought Kennedy, the government, and the FBI hated unions in the 1950's. In their opinion, it was because unions represented the single biggest threat to the super wealthy power structure. If labor had a say in their wages, the playing field would begin to even out. They said Hoffa symbolized their struggle to achieve the American dream.

We were stunned by their staunch support for Hoffa, who had a known reputation of using illegal business practices including bribery, extortion, and coercion. He was also known to have strong mafia ties. The public didn't care about that, but related to the salaries he and the unions brought into their households.

The program aired on stations in Detroit, Philadelphia, and Los Angeles, being the highest rated program in the 13 year run of our series.

When the program was replayed four weeks later, we asked for public opinion and thousands responded. More that half the calls stated that the government was working for rich people and didn't care about the plight of the working class.

With the success of these programs, I began receiving

access to national news stories on nearly every event, including new government disclosures about Marilyn Monroe. For the next ten years, all reports from Associated Press and other international news agencies came to our production company.

My boss, Peter Newell, a Vice President with the company, encouraged the producers to cover national stories and conventions to give a minority perspective on the subject matter. Our views on Marilyn Monroe and Jimmy Hoffa were perfect examples of what he was talking about. Incidentally, Capital Cities turned five radio and some small market television stations into assets which would later be used to purchase the holdings of the American Broadcasting Company, ABC Network.

CHAPTER 8:
Extra, Extra, The Empire Strikes Back

Nearly 15 years had passed since the death of Marilyn Monroe. Still, there hadn't been any type of big push for a new investigation. Although a few friends and some of her fans were crying foul, for the most part she was still simply a 'probable suicide'. However, the radio programs ignited a small spark, becoming a catalyst in the search for Marilyn's true cause of death.

In the time following our highly successful Hoffa show, I stepped up my investigation of the facts surrounding the Monroe case. Meeting Bob had really stimulated my research efforts, which primarily consisted of gathering newspaper articles, magazine clippings, and audiotapes that shed light on what I knew about the case. During that time, Bob and I would talk occasionally over the phone to compare notes and clarify details about her death.

One Saturday, I was conducting a production workshop for interns at KPOL-AM in Hollywood. The offices were normally empty on the weekend, so I knew most of the people who belonged there. While walking downstairs, I noticed a man who hurriedly ducked through a door. His face was not familiar, so I walked over to see if I could help him with anything. He claimed to be a salesman for the station, there to retrieve some papers from his desk.

He then darted quickly out the back door, nothing in his hands and left. Not thinking much, I continued on with my task. About an hour later, while leaving the station, a car came across Sunset Boulevard, jumped the curb and struck the building, nearly hitting me in the process. I was shaken as I watched the wrecked car back out and speed away.

The police were called, but could only conclude that a drunk driver ran a red light and lost control of the car. When the report was filed, little attention was given to the fact that the car failed to stop, had left the scene, and was aimed right at me. Thankfully, my athletic skills allowed me to get off the sidewalk before being planted on the hood of that car. It was a very scary situation that was way too close for comfort. A little closer and I could have been killed.

Was this just an accident and nothing to be alarmed about? There was no way to tell, but later that evening there was another strange car parked on my street when I arrived home. It appeared two men were sitting inside the vehicle. Maybe it was just paranoia, because there wasn't any real evidence that someone was stalking me, was there? It made me wonder, who was that man I saw at the radio station earlier? He was definitely out of place.

My kids were visiting for the weekend, so I packed a few

things and we spent the night at my mother's. I had been divorced from my wife for about 10 years, but maintained a great relationship with my 3 vacation breaking youngsters. They were teenagers now, and worked with me at the radio station when they could, covering stories for the radio program.

Lionel Jr., Crystal, and Lance. Even at such a young age, they were veterans at covering high profile stories such as Los Angeles Mayor Thomas Bradley's Inauguration and the SLA kidnapping of Patricia Hearst. Because of their association with the show, they were fortunate to meet some of the most notable African-American figures of the time. Muhammad Ali, Andrew Young, Brock Peters, and Nancy Wilson are all people featured in shows they helped produce.

We would get together, usually once a month, to have something we called family talks. During that time, we would discuss everything going on in our lives and share whatever feelings we had. It was a very special period, which has kept us all extremely close throughout the years.

We had discussed the Marilyn Monroe case many times during our talks, both when they were younger and since the radio program. However, things were moving fast and I wanted them to be aware of what was happening around them. Bob was talking about trying to get a grand jury investigation, and this would have major implications. From what I had read in the diary, I knew there would be some ruffled feathers if the grand jury got involved. Strange things were already going on around me, and if I was going to continue with this, my kids needed to know everything. That's the reason we had family talks, and that's the way we were.

After explaining things to them, my oldest son Lionel, who was at the radio station at the time of the incident, asked me a question.

"Why do you think it's so important to talk about Marilyn Monroe now?"

I thought about it for a moment before answering.

"Son, I really only had two choices. Say nothing and let the information die with me or tell the world what I know. I've been holding on to this story for a long time, but people need to hear it. This is the right thing to do."

"Well, if people really need to hear it, why don't you write a book like Bob and tell your story?" My daughter Crystal asked.

"If you guys help me organize my notes and research, maybe I will," I said thoughtfully.

From that point on, they wanted to know every detail of my experiences with the Marilyn Monroe case. They began to gather all my notes and organize the investigative evidence I had collected. That would become the early origins of my memoirs.

Still somewhat concerned about keeping us protected, I decided to get some advice. Captain Edward Rasheed was the man Malcolm X had introduced me to in 1962. I remembered the calming force he had been during the Watts riots as a member of the Nation of Islam's famed security force called the "Fruit Of Islam". He was someone I had become well acquainted with, having worked with him on several television projects for the organization.   He knew everything there was to know about security. Even more importantly, I trusted him.

The Nation of Islam was viewed as a mysterious group, but to the African-American community, they were like guardians. I was quite comfortable, talking to Rasheed, and he asked me to explain what happened. Not sure where to begin, I explained the Marilyn Monroe situation and what happened at the radio station. He asked if I filed a police report, which the station had already been done. Captain Rasheed told me not to worry about it, and that they would take care of the rest.

My investigation with Bob Slatzer was becoming more intense as the months went by. Many new details about Marilyn's death were continuing to surface and Bob was moving full speed ahead to get County Officials to launch a grand jury investigation into her case. During that time, I had began producing a television show at KVST-TV 68, which was a local PBS affiliated station in Hollywood.

When Bob discovered I was producing the show, he mentioned we could receive great exposure by producing a TV show about Marilyn's case.   At the time, I hadn't thought about it much, but he was right. When I mentioned it to the team, they were ecstatic and a production date was set.

Bob also informed me that Fred Otash, one of the men who wiretapped Marilyn's house, would agree to appear on the program. With that revelation, all of a sudden this had turned into something huge. Otash was a major witness who claimed to still possess audiotapes from the night Marilyn died.

When the production day arrived, the studio was buzzing like never before. Bob arrived extra early, like he always did, and we began prepping for the shoot. He mentioned being concerned that Otash hadn't answered his phone all day, but said he knew the time and location.

While getting things ready in the control booth, we began to hear a commotion in the studio. My youngest son Lance came running in.

"Dad, there's something bad happening out there." I told him to wait in the booth with Bob and walked over to the door, cautiously cracking it open.

Three men had busted in and began threatening the crew, throwing chairs and waving a gun. It was unclear what they wanted because their actions were so erratic. Standing there, looking in disbelief, I saw someone tackle the man holding the gun in almost a blur, forcing him to drop it. They scuffled for a few seconds, and then all three ran out the studio door. The scene was absolutely unreal.

Hurrying over to see if everyone was alright, I noticed it

was a member of Captain Rasheed's FOI security team who had disarmed the man. Mind you, I had not mentioned this shoot to Rasheed at all. When I inquired about who told him to be here he answered,

"The Captain said you might need our help today and to keep an eye on things."

We promptly called the police and turned the gun over to them. Talking to Rasheed turned out to be a smart move.

I never really knew what that whole situation was about. The three men were never found and after filing the police report, we never heard anything about the incident again. The truth is, only two facts remained about that entire experience. One was that we were unable to produce that television show, which would have been game changing at that time, and two, Fred Otash never showed up to the shoot and never agreed to appear again. Maybe this was just a random event, but my instincts always told me it was something much more sinister. Certainly however, I was fortunate to have those protectors of the peace and thanked God for Edward Rasheed.

In 1978, I agreed to hold a press conference in Los Angeles. It was the first time my story would be revealed to the public. We knew this would have major consequences, but Bob was convinced it would gain us the publicity we needed to get the grand jury involved in Marilyn's case.

We also decided to enlist the help of Sergeant Jack Clemmons, formerly with the Los Angeles Police

Department. Jack Clemmons was the first police officer on the scene when Marilyn's death was reported. Bob had interviewed him while writing his book and he provided vivid details about the LAPD cover-up that took place at the crime scene. We knew that his testimony would weigh heavily when presenting our case to the media.

While conducting my official Coroner's investigation in 1962, I had spoken with Jack about the case. When we finally got together and talked, he remembered our conversation, saying it had always been his hope that the truth about Marilyn would be revealed. Jack always seemed like a straight shooter. He told it like it was. Speaking with him again after all these years convinced me more than ever that I was doing the right thing. Our experiences with the case shared many similarities and he too had a burning desire to set the facts straight.

Together, the three of us agreed to stand side by side and make the public aware of how intricate this Marilyn Monroe conspiracy was. We believed getting a grand jury investigation was an obtainable goal and the press conference was just the beginning. The road ahead would be long for this improbable journey, but nevertheless, it was a path we were all about to embark on.

You can't imagine the anxiety we felt, leading up to the press conference. The story I was about to reveal would accuse and possibly incriminate the former Coroner of Los Angeles in the concealment of Marilyn's true cause of death.

Although Dr. Curphey and I had difficulties in the past, this wasn't any type of vendetta. All I wanted to do was tell the truth about how the Coroner's office handled the case. My biggest concern was the repercussions, and what they would be.

The press release announced that the Deputy Coroner who investigated the death of Marilyn Monroe would tell the story of the inconsistencies that occurred in the Coroner's Office. Sergeant Jack Clemmons of the police department would tell why the LAPD failed to investigate evidence of a conspiracy at her house. Bob Slatzer would reveal evidence that Bobby Kennedy had been at her house the night she died and discuss Marilyn's planned press conference.

Something else also concerned me about this press conference. It was the diary. Since my ordeal at the Coroner's office, the only person outside of my family, which the diary had been discussed with, was Bob. Although my reason for being there had nothing to do with the book, what if I was asked about it? That possibility had to be considered, along with what my response would be.

Since comparing notes with Slatzer, at least I knew more about the circumstances surrounding what Marilyn had written about and the Government Agencies she was involved with. My understanding of the things I read was much clearer. My decision was to answer any specific questions about her diary. It was finally time to throw my fate into the wind.

There were about 15 or so microphones and numerous hot lights at the podium. I stood there for what seemed like an eternity as we all made statements and answered questions from the press. While cameras and tape recorders rolled, we each told our unique stories, trying to remain cool, calm, and collected.

Jack told of the LAPD's role in the cover-up. He stated that his initial crime scene investigation report was completely ignored by his supervisors. He continued in saying that key witnesses had completely changed their stories about the night's events. He mentioned that upon his arrival to the scene, the housekeeper Eunice Murray had told him that the body was found at 12:30am. When detectives did their follow-up report, that time was changed to 3:30am.

Jack also revealed she was in a room with numerous empty pill bottles on the bedside table. The two doctors, Greenson and Engelberg, and the housekeeper all told different stories about the night's events and appeared nervous. It was my first time hearing details about the bedroom the star was discovered in, since no police report was part of my official case files.

Jack went on to say that when he arrived at the house, he noticed Marilyn was lying face down in the bed and had been dead for some time. Deputy Coroner Danbacker had also reported her time of death being incorrect and observed evidence suggesting the body had been moved. That information was never noted in the preliminary autopsy or

Suicide Team reports.

Jack stated that when he made his report available to his superiors, it was disregarded. When he broke LAPD policy and told a news reporter what he knew, he was suspended and later fired.

Bob responded to all questions about the Kennedys' involvement in her case. He revealed what he knew about the wire tapers and discussed his close relationship with Marilyn. His disclosure about Robert Kennedy being at her house the night she died dominated the press conference. Bob had written extensively about Marilyn's connection with the Kennedys and members of the news media had questions. He also talked about Marilyn's planned press conference and discussed the existence of her diary. Bob told the press he had seen the book and that's what she was going reveal before she died.

My account of the activities within the Los Angeles County Coroner's Office brought into scrutiny the Coroner's handling of the case. In my statement, I discussed Dr. Curphey's treatment of the investigation, missing police documents, changing of medical documents, and the Suicide Investigation Team's findings.

The press wanted to know why I signed a death certificate declaring Marilyn's death to be probable suicide. I described how Dr. Curphey demanded I sign off and close the case. That announcement seemed to catch everyone off guard and perhaps set the tone for things to come.

Although a little nervous, I felt comfortable answering questions about the case of Marilyn Monroe, and what happened at the Coroner's Office. Finally, a reporter asked whether Jack or I had seen Marilyn's diary. Jack said no, but my response was that her diary had been logged in as property at the Los Angeles County Coroner's Office. I told them her diary was in my possession while conducting the official investigation, having read parts of it during that time.

The reporter quickly followed up with what was in the diary. I explained she made numerous references regarding John Kennedy, Robert Kennedy, and U.S. Intelligence Agencies. I told them Marilyn wrote many pages about her experiences with them, but nothing that would implicate any conspirators in her murder.

After the press conference, I left for home, emotionally drained. My experience in front of the news media had been incredibly intense. As expected, reporters began calling the Coroner's Office for their response. Dr. Curphey had retired as Chief Coroner in 1967, and Dr. Noguchi had replaced him. Noguchi couldn't deny my assessment of the facts and choose to talk about the case based upon the Suicide Investigation Team's evaluation. He couldn't explain why so many documents had changed, how Marilyn's tissue samples had disappeared, or why Dr. Curphey had ordered me to close the case.

Most local television stations and newspapers ran stories on the press conference, but the broadcast networks and national publications didn't mention much about the Kennedy connection. Bob was extremely disappointed. Exposing Robert Kennedy's involvement with Marilyn was central to him. Bob believed it was that immersion that got her killed.

During the next few days, I kept a low profile and took some time to evaluate what had just happened. My oldest son Lionel, who attended the press conference, called saying how surprised he was about the high amount of coverage it received. I remember telling him that being in the spotlight was something I never anticipated and my thoughts were mixed about the entire situation. The truth of the matter was, if the whole thing had went away right then and there, I wouldn't have been mad at all. However, little did we know that a fuse had been lit and our story was about to explode nationwide.

About a week later, Bob called incredibly excited. He told me the producers of the hit series "In Search Of" had called and wanted us to appear on the program. It was the number one television newsmagazine in the country, with widespread international appeal. This was a momentous opportunity to get national exposure for Marilyn's case.

Bob, Jack, and myself were interviewed on the circumstances surrounding her death and about the Kennedys' involvement in the cover up. We each told our stories in as much detail as possible. For the first time, I provided elaborate information about Marilyn's diary, what was in it and how it disappeared from the Coroner's office. The entire episode was dedicated to the Marilyn Monroe death.

Leonard Nemoy, of Star Trek fame, was host of the program, and as it turned out, a friend of the Kennedy family. He objected to the Robert Kennedy implications and demanded that it be edited out. The producers bowed to Nemoy's demand and the references were never aired. The episode however, was an enormous hit. "The Death of Marilyn Monroe" was one of the highest rated ever for the "In Search Of" series, but it was now apparent that the Kennedys' influence still packed a powerful punch.

Interview requests began flooding in from news media around the world. I had never quite realized the full extent of Marilyn's popularity across the globe until then. Even the Italian Television Network traveled half way around the world just to interview us. Our story had gone world wide in the blink of an eye.

Quite naturally, The National Enquirer was the first news publication to show interest in the Marilyn-Robert Kennedy love affair. They requested Bob and I to grant them an interview discussing the facts surrounding her death, Kennedy's involvement, and what was in the diary. Although Bob was elated, I had doubts about giving them my story. The National Enquirer was considered a tabloid magazine and my goal was never to make this a gossip story. Most of the people I knew did not hold the publication in high esteem, however, this was obviously important to Bob so I granted the interview.

Our campaign had created quite a stir with the public. Now all of her friends and acquaintances were calling the Coroner, Police, and District Attorney, demanding a new investigation into Marilyn's death. What I had not realized was that when Bob Slatzer found me, a missing part of the puzzle appeared. I gave his investigation the added credibility needed to be heard by County officials. With a Deputy Coroner set to testify on the Coroner's role in the cover-up, the grand jury would have no choice but to open the case.

In the midst of all this, someone claiming to be former Deputy Coroner Danbacker called Bob. The man had a heavy European accent, as did Danbacker, and apparently had been following the attention we were receiving. He claimed to have been in hiding, and had something important for our investigation.

When I told Bob how significant of a role he had played, his ears perked up. Danbacker was the one that brought her property into the Coroner's Office and had spent three or four hours searching her house for medical information. The diary and press release was included in the property he retrieved from the house.

The only person on the staff who might have been able to put a little light on Marilyn's personal property was Deputy Coroner Danbacker. I often wondered what else he may have seen in the house, and how much he knew about what was in the diary. He would've had to look inside the book to determine its relevance.

Bob told me Danbacker sounded nervous and asked if any money was available. Bob thought he was talking about the diary, but said he never was specific. They arranged a meeting near Bakersfield, which is about 100 miles north of Los Angeles, and Bob made the drive to meet with him. Arriving to the location, he turned onto a dirt road, which led to a section of oil pumps. There were a few workers and a couple of trucks in the area so he parked near one of the pumps and got out.

After waiting over an hour for him to come, it started to get dark and Bob said he began to get nervous. The workers in the area were leaving and he noticed a car parked down the road, which he thought might have been Danbacker. However, two men stepped out and began talking, and then another car pulled-up and parked behind them. These men didn't have uniforms on or fit the image of workers in an oil field. Bob said he left and drove back to Los Angeles, wondering what had just happened and looking in the rear view mirror to see if any one was following him. He never heard from this man claiming to be Danbacker again.

Los Angeles County Officials began taking note of our claims. I was formally requested to share my story at a hearing in front of the Los Angeles County Board of Supervisors. They had become interested in Marilyn's case and were considering requesting an official grand jury investigation. This is what we all had been working for. The County Board of Supervisors oversaw the activities of the Los Angeles County Coroner and had the power to get a grand jury convened. After presenting my story to them, the Board thanked me for coming forward and voted to begin the process for opening a grand jury investigation to determine the facts.

However, something funny happened along the way. Los Angeles District Attorney John Van de Camp decided to initiate his own Marilyn Monroe Inquiry, independent of the Board of Supervisors. Van de Camp, who was aware of the eminent grand jury investigation at the time, made the announcement less than a week after I spoke to the Board.

In 1962, the Los Angeles District Attorney's office warned me not to mention the book to anyone, and now I had told everything to the County Board of Supervisors. Hoping this was just some strange coincidence, I called Bob to see what he knew about it. He said the word is out that Van de Camp wants to take control of this Investigation and the grand jury will wait to see what he comes up with.

I had jumped right back in the frying pan and the fire was on high. I knew the DA's office had no intention of saying the Coroner's Office had been in possession of a book that contained information on Marilyn Monroe's death. So why were they opening this Threshold Inquiry? Were they trying to cover-up the cover-up? Things were getting out of control and there was no way to be prepared for what was coming next.

John Van de Camp assembled a team of investigators led by his highly touted Assistant District Attorney Ronald 'Mike' Carroll. The team began making arrangements to speak with all key witnesses, who were involved with Marilyn's case, including me.

Almost immediately, swarms of reporters converged on my house, their news trucks completely shutting down the neighborhood. Apparently the D.A.'s Office had released sealed documents from my criminal case in 1962. They made all case evidence against me available to the media, mounting an all out assault on my credibility.

Just like they did in 1962, the media had a field day while presenting this one sided story. KNBC in Los Angeles ran it locally on their evening newscast, and it seemed as if everyone I knew saw it. Although most people understood the type of person I really was and supported me, the impact was still hurtful. Bob suggested we hold a press conference to offer my side of the story, which was something I didn't want to do. That criminal case in 62' was a life-changing incident I thought was buried forever. It was my only criminal encounter with the law and those records had been sealed since 1969.

Years earlier, Bob once shared with me that threats were made against his life and character if he included details about Marilyn's involvement with the Kennedys in his book. Maybe I should have paid better attention to what he was saying. Real or imagined, there was a sense of uneasiness that could not be ignored while being involved with this highly sensitive case. Now I was about to come face to face with a Los Angeles District Attorney, who obviously had it in for me. Add to that my recent life endangering encounters, I could only conclude that my situation was extremely precarious.

CHAPTER 9:
The District Attorney

The Los Angeles District Attorney's office began their inquiry to investigate the possible murder of Marilyn Monroe by a person or persons unknown. Some twenty years after her death, because of the publicity we created, Assistant District Attorney Ronald Carroll was commissioned to determine whether a homicide investigation was justified. His proclaimed mission was to uncover all the facts surrounding Marilyn's death.

Most people were elated about this D.A. inquiry, but my feelings were understandably different. Think about it, if the District Attorney's office didn't want me talking about the diary in 1962, then they didn't want the truth. Even more significant, if Carroll knew the real story, what would he do with it?

To be honest, this D.A.'s inquiry had caught me completely off guard. Our aim had always been the grand jury, and it never dawned on me that I could end up right back in front of the District Attorney. Obviously the fact that nearly twenty years had passed made no difference.

Bob convinced me that a press conference would be in my best interest. He said a private investigator from the Nick Harris Detective Agency, named Milo Speriglio, had uncovered some FBI disclosures on the wiretaps at Marilyn's house. We could issue a joint press release and combine the press conference to serve both purposes.

We held the press conference a few weeks later. Telling my story about why I left the Coroner's Office was very difficult. The press grilled me, but fortunately, Speriglio's wiretap information diverted some of the questions. Afterwards, a Deputy District Attorney from Ronald Carroll's inquiry team approached and said they needed to speak with me. He asked could I meet with them for lunch at the Los Angeles County Criminal Courts Building to answer some questions.

Although completely shocked at being asked, I agreed and left to meet with him after the press conference. Upon arriving downtown, I was met by three distinguished looking individuals who asked me to follow them.

We went to a place I can only describe as the dungeons of the Court House. The interview room looked like a place where serious interrogations were conducted. It was dark and surrounded by glass behind which people could watch or tape the proceedings. Quite frankly, it looked like a place out of the movies.

There was no hint of coffee or tea or anything that represented lunch. It was kind of intimidating, but not completely unexpected. It was obvious they hadn't forgot about 1962, and I felt all this was to let me know. I sat there alone in the room for good while before anybody came in. Sitting there was one of the coldest experiences of my life. The thoughts running across my mind were out of control. Finally the door opened, and three men walked in. Shutting the door behind them, they stood there and looked at me. After the silent pause, one of them walked over and introduced himself as Assistant District Attorney Ronald Carroll.

Carroll was a man with a strange combination of intensity and humor. From the moment he walked into the interrogation room, it was apparent he didn't like me. Carroll's overall attitude was testy, but he readily joked with the two men sitting beside him. The whole situation was designed to intimidate and put me on edge. But I had seen it all before. When I was 22 years old, it was easy to be bullied by a District Attorney with a hidden agenda. However, things were different now. No matter what tricks they pulled from out of their sleeves, I was going to tell the truth about what happened to Marilyn, and if there were consequences to that, so be it.

I was asked multiple questions about the activities that transpired at the Coroner's Office. We went over why it was my belief her death wasn't suicide. He showed me the revised version of Marilyn's case files, which disputed much of what I was saying. Looking at the files, the first thing I noticed was that many of the Deputy's names were misspelled, and some did not work for the Coroner's Office 1962. I pointed that out to Carroll and told him that this was not the original paperwork from Marilyn's case.

Taking the documents back from me, Carroll said,

"I'll check on that, but these are the files we have."

When I told Carroll about the diary and its contents, he said the original D.A.'s report quoted Dr. Ralph Greenson, Dr. Myron Engelberg, and other unnamed associates, saying they never saw a diary and doubted whether, in her final months especially, Monroe was capable of keeping one.

Carroll told me that in his opinion, there wasn't any reason to believe a diary ever existed. A little irritated, I snapped back at him by saying that not only did the diary exist, but I also gave investigators from his office this same information twenty years ago. Check your records, I told him, but don't sit there and say there isn't any reason to believe a diary existed.

Perhaps a little stunned by my mini tirade, he replied,

"We are going to get to the bottom of this."

I was definitely a little aggravated at the situation, because we had come too far for this type of treatment. It was imperative that Mr. Carroll understood what the facts were. His attitude did not even matter at this point. There was no controlling what he would do with the information, but I was going make sure he heard it. The rest was up to him.

When the interview was complete, I was asked not to mention what was discussed until after the investigation was final. They also asked me would I being willing to take a lie detector test, which was agreed to. After telling my lawyer, he requested the list of questions be submitted as a condition of me taking the polygraph. The investigators never responded, and no test was ever scheduled.

Sergeant Jack Clemmons also visited the District Attorneys Office during the inquiry. Jack informed us that Carroll and his investigators harassed him the entire time he was there. Jack said he tried to tell his account of how the housekeeper changed her story, but they were convinced he had misunderstood her. They acted as if he was incompetent, and he told us at one point an investigator joked that he was hallucinating. Carroll said they didn't place much weight on his statements because he wasn't a trained LAPD homicide investigator and had no experience in suicides.

Jack said he left the D.A.'s office thinking the Inquiry was a sham and the District Attorney wasn't seriously trying to investigate Marilyn's death. He believed they already had their minds made up and the interviews were just a formality. Jack never expected the treatment he received and was seriously shaken by his experience at the Inquiry. We both managed to have a little laugh when I shared with him my experience.

The next witness was another man I first met in 1962, Los Angeles County Deputy District Attorney, John Miner. He had been the first to notify Dr. Curphey of problems in Marilyn's cause of death. Miner informed investigators of what he had told Dr. Curphey about meeting with her psychiatrist Dr. Ralph Greenson, who told him that Marilyn would not have committed suicide. Miner claimed that Greenson played audiotapes for him that Monroe made in the days before she died. What he heard proved to him the actress was anything but suicidal. However, Greenson played these recordings with the condition Miner would never reveal their contents.

Subsequently, Miner refused to disclose what was on the tapes and Carroll concluded his statements did not warrant any further investigation. The resulting report stated that because of discrepancies and unanswered questions, Miner's statements would be left out of the final report.

As the investigation went on, the District Attorney spoke with numerous witnesses and experts while trying to gather what they called 'relevant facts'. Carroll acknowledged that key evidence was destroyed, leaving many questions unanswered. Monroe's internist, Dr. Hyman Engelberg, told the D.A.'s investigators that he had prescribed the medications that could have killed her.

But the fact remained that none of the other medications that Dr. Engelberg prescribed was found in her body. No questions were asked about how the police handled the many drug containers found at the house nor why the containers that did arrive at the Coroner's Office, were empty. No answer was obtained as to where they came from or who brought them into Marilyn's room. More importantly, who had tried to get the body away from her house to hide the facts?

Most of the people who came forward with information on Marilyn's death did so willingly, although there were some who did not wish to get involved. The only public officials willing to make statements to the Inquiry were Jack Clemmons, John Miner, and myself. Together, we represented the Police Department, District Attorney, and Coroner's Office for the County and/or City of Los Angeles. All three of us agreed that a cover-up had taken place and that it involved each of these departments. All of us had witnessed evidence being ignored, mishandled, changed, or manipulated during the original investigation and our opinion was that Marilyn Monroe did not commit suicide.

A few months later, Carroll and the District Attorney's Office issued a 30-page report, stating in part "Our inquiries and document examination uncovered no credible evidence supporting a murder theory." Despite all the testimonies, Carroll said he did not find any credible evidence that the Coroner's Office was ever in possession of a diary. He placed little or no weight to the fact that key witnesses changed their story to police officers nor that Marilyn's psychiatrist had informed a Deputy District Attorney that she was not suicidal.

The DA investigators made several reports on Marilyn's relations with the mafia. One member of the team, Frank Hronek, believed she was murdered, and suspected Sam Giancana and Johnny Roselli were involved with her death. In one report he wrote,

"Marilyn might have been killed to keep her silent and further investigation was necessary." His final conclusion said, "Associating herself with the mafia was dangerous because of her connection with the Kennedys." Despite the fact this was Carroll's own investigator making the claim, he chose not to pursue it any further.

Carroll concluded that a murder of Monroe, fitting the known facts of her death, would have required a massive conspiracy. The Conclusion of the District Attorney review was that Marilyn Monroe acted alone in her suicide and there was no evidence to support that anyone assisted her.

Four months after the investigation began, John Van de Camp, who was running for State Attorney General, closed down the probe. Not surprisingly, one of the largest contributors and supporters to his election campaign was Senator Ted Kennedy. Van De Camp went on to win the election, and became State Attorney General. The Marilyn probe was buried along our hopes for a grand jury investigation.

Once again, the circumstances surrounding Marilyn Monroe's death would be swept under the rug. This Inquiry, along with the other investigative probes, was just another part of the so-called massive conspiracy to cover-up evidence in the case. A cover up that included the involvement of President John Kennedy, Attorney General Robert Kennedy, F.B.I. Director J. Edgar Hoover, C.I.A. operatives James O'Connell and Robert Maheu, Teamster Leader Jimmy Hoffa, Mafia Leader Sam Giancana, Dr. Myron Engelberg, and Dr. Ralph Greenson.

Bob, Jack, and I were extremely disappointed at the way all of this had unfolded. The Inquiry and everything that happened leading up to it had been a gut-wrenching experience. Over the next few months, my head was filled with confusing thoughts about everything that had transpired. Personally, I was ready for Marilyn Monroe to go away once more and things getting back to normal.

Not surprisingly, Bob wasn't going to let that happen. In fact, he seemed to be feeling rather optimistic about our situation. He insisted if he laid this investigation out one more time, in front of the County Board of Supervisors, they could still be persuaded to bypass the District Attorney's Office and request the grand jury investigation.

Bob began to assemble what he called the Marilyn Files. Every single bit of evidence or information associated with Marilyn's death was to be compiled into one comprehensive investigation. Bob already owned, what looked to be, the largest collection of material anywhere relating to Marilyn's case. His plan was to create one concise report, containing the most up to date facts, and present it to the County Board of Supervisors.

Although I never fully understood why Bob was on this crusade, you had to admire his work ethic. His best-selling book, "The Life and Curious Death of Marilyn Monroe" was the best literary work available on the Hollywood starlet during that time. Bob was a true champion for Marilyn, who would never rest until justice was served and never would he give up the search for new evidence.

Bob talked about discovering a man named James Hall, who claimed to have driven an ambulance that visited Marilyn's house the night of her death. Hall was working for Schaffer Ambulance Service at the time, and allegedly arrived at the scene after responding to a radio call.

Upon his arrival to her house, James Hall claimed the team found Marilyn lying on the bed face up. He said they quickly moved her to the floor, slightly dropping her in their haste then beginning to apply CPR. At that point he insist Marilyn was still alive, but this is where his account got strange.

Hall told a perplexing story about a man, claiming to be Marilyn's doctor, who arrived and injected some kind of serum into her heart with a syringe. The doctor, who he later identified as Ralph Greenson then pronounced her dead and the ambulance team was told they could leave. Having worked numerous emergency cases, Hall said the CPR was working, and she could have been saved.

James Hall took two or three lie detector tests to validate his claim. According to Jack Clemmons, one of the tests was with the so-called creator of the polygraph machine. Hall passed all these tests. In a recorded interview, the owner of Schafer's Ambulance Service also confirmed that one of their vehicles was sent to the house that night to pick up Mrs. Monroe. Her neighbors also validated this account.

I was never certain about Jim Hall's story, although we spoke about the incident a few times. Having seen Marilyn's body and talking with John Miner and Dr. Noguchi, there was no evidence of a needle mark on her chest. However, to my knowledge, only Noguchi and Miner were at the autopsy and with the way this case had gone thus far, anything was possible.

One thing was certain, this scenario could also account for there being no poison left in the stomach. It also magnifies the importance of Marilyn's tissue samples being destroyed by Dr. Abernathy under orders from Dr. Curphey. These samples could have provided concrete evidence of what really killed her.

As Bob began to develop the Marilyn Files, the first thing he did was connect the updated evidence with the chain of events for that night.

Eunice Murray, the housekeeper, first told Sergeant Jack

Clemmons that she discovered the body at about 12:30am. She later told LAPD detectives and the Coroner's Office that time was 3:30 AM. She reported being awakened then seeing Marilyn's light on and becoming alarmed when she discovered the door was locked. She then called Dr. Greenson. When he arrived, they broke her bedroom window, climbed in, and discovered she was dead.

Dr. Greenson removed the phone from Marilyn's hand, immediately calling Dr. Engelberg and Peter Lawford. According to the official police report, at 3:45am Dr. Engelberg arrived to find Marilyn face down on the bed and pronounced her dead at 3:50am. According to Clemmons' story, there were at least 4-5 hours unaccounted for between the times Mrs. Murray found Marilyn and when the doctors called the police. It was not until 4:25am that the Los Angeles Police Department was called about the death. Clemmons said when he took their initial statements, he asked the doctors why it took so long to notify the police, and was told they had to notify the movie studio first.

The police investigation into the death of Marilyn Monroe began like a routine inquiry into an unnatural death. Sergeant Clemmons began by examining the bedroom. According to this veteran LAPD officer, everything in her room appeared to be staged. He specifically noticed the prescription bottles, and her body, looked as though they had been skillfully placed.

Jack was also very familiar with overdose fatalities and

knew bodies would always contort from the convulsions that come with this type of death. That wasn't the case with Marilyn. Her body was lying very naturally on the bed, appearing to have been deceased for a long period of time. In Jack's opinion as a trained officer of the law, the whole room, or crime scene as he called it, looked "out of place." After obtaining statements from everyone present, he left when detectives arrived and Sergeant R.E. Byron eventually assumed responsibility.

Byron overlooked significant contradictions and gaps in the witnesses' stories. Fingerprints were lifted and photographs were taken, but physical evidence at the scene was completely ignored and the entire basis of what happened that night was premised on statements made by Dr. Greenson, Dr. Engelberg, and housekeeper Eunice Murray. According to Clemmons, when he arrived to the house that early Sunday morning, these three were acting extremely suspicious and had a difficult time getting their story straight.

Finally, the body was brought to the Coroner's office, but not before the studio tried to get it released to the mortuary without being examined by the Coroner. The preliminary toxicology report said 30 Nembutal were found in her throat, but none in her stomach. That report is later changed along with other key documents. Then there was the rush to close the case by Los Angeles County Coroner Dr. Theodore Curphey and, of course, the removal of

Marilyn's diary, containing all her notes about the Kennedys, CIA, FBI and the mafia.

When Bob finished assembling these Marilyn Files, the information was absolutely overwhelming. In 1985, he presented his report and petitioned the L.A. County Board of Supervisors to re-open the inquiry into Marilyn's death.

Slatzer's passionate plea to the Board of Supervisors was powerful. Board Members also heard written statements from one of Marilyn's best friends, Jeanne Carmine. In 1982, Carmen spoke to Ronald Carroll's investigators during the D.A.'s Inquiry and provided them a detailed account of Marilyn's diary.

Jeanne Carmine had seen the book and told investigators how Marilyn had shared many intimate details about her writings. Carmen said the diary contained sensitive information about Marilyn's relationship with both Kennedys, along with her involvement with the Central Intelligence Agency. She was aware of the meetings between John Kennedy and Mafia members, from entries in the diary.

Carmine claimed the diary posed a major threat to Marilyn and others. Her love affair with Bobby Kennedy was all she wrote about in her final days. Carmine also described the evening, she, Kennedy, and Marilyn were at Monroe's house and Kennedy discovered the diary. She claimed he examined it and became upset. He told Marilyn she should never put anything in writing and to throw the diary away. Carmine stated that Kennedy did not take the diary and she did not know what Monroe did with it.

Surprisingly, Jeanne Carmine's statements were omitted from Ronald Carroll's final Inquiry report. Other than Bob and myself, this was the first time someone had come forward and testified that Marilyn had documented the last years of her life. Now three people were telling of her association with the CIA and other federal agencies. In all of our opinions, this book had been well constructed and revealed more than just a failed relationship with the Kennedys.

Carmine and Slatzer both knew Marilyn when she was alive and had seen the diary. An official recommendation was given to the Los Angeles County Grand Jury to launch a preliminary investigation into the facts surrounding Marilyn's death. When the request was given to the Grand Jury body, they unanimously agreed to begin a new inquiry.

Hearing that news was a remarkable feeling. After all we had endured, through this unbelievable process, each of us felt a sincere sense of satisfaction, and nobody was more thrilled than Bob. When I saw him, the smile on his face was lighting the room and I was happy for him.

Grand Jury foreman Sam Cordova launched the preliminary investigation, which would determine whether a full-scale investigation was warranted. Cordoba looked at evidence no other public official would ever touch and asked questions about the contradictory statements that witnesses had given. Cordova looked like a knight in shining armor for

Marilyn's justice.

The Grand Jury Foreman scheduled a press conference and made this announcement,

"There is enough evidence to substantiate a special prosecutor to work with the Grand Jury on the investigation. A full-scale investigation has never been done by the Grand Jury. People have not testified under oath and that should have been done a long time ago. It should have been done in 1962."

However, the D.A.'s Office had other ideas once again. Ira Reiner was the newly elected District Attorney, and in an unprecedented action, he removed Grand Jury Foreman Sam Cordova from his position, effectively firing him. No grand jury foreman in California history had ever been removed from office. It was a move that sent political vibrations around the country.

In addition to that, Ira Reiner announced the District Attorney's office would once again launch an investigation their own. One of Reiner's investigators contacted me and asked would I come to their office. As incredible as it seemed, I was heading back in front of the District Attorney once again.

"Returning to the District Attorney's office was the last thing I wanted," I thought 'as I entered the building and walked up to their office. However, everything seemed like it was crumbling once again, and if talking to the D.A. could help, it was worth a try. Still, I could not forget the treatment received a few years earlier by one of Reiner's predecessors, so my guard was definitely up.

The second interview took place in the District Attorney's Office, where at least there was sunlight. Things were completely different this time.

"Thanks for coming Mr. Grandison" is how I was greeted.

The D. A. investigators were now giving some attention to my claim that Marilyn Monroe kept a journal. They were aware of what Jeanne Carmine had been saying, and wanted to know more about the contents of this mysterious book.

Reiner's investigator was very polite and listened attentively to my story.

"Don't worry Mr. Grandison, you're going to get your investigation," he said as he helped me put on my coat when I prepared to leave.

Leaving the office, I felt extremely positive about our situation. Maybe Ira Reiner really wanted to clean up the D.A.'s office and give Marilyn Monroe the investigation she deserved. However, that was not to be the case.

The next day newspaper headlines read,

"New Marilyn Probe Nixed by D.A."

And just like that, everything was over.

I had to come to grips with the fact that the cover-up was still in full effect. Someone didn't want the public or anyone else to know the depths of this matter. With the Kennedy's,

CIA and the FBI involved, any official public investigation into the Marilyn Monroe's death was doomed by the so-called massive conspiracy theory from the start. With these power brokers involved, nobody else was taken seriously and neither testimony nor evidence was viewed as fact.

For all intent and purposes, this was the end of law enforcement's attempt to uncover the truth. There were more promises of District Attorney Reviews and mutterings of convening a grand jury. Not surprisingly, even as County officials stopped their investigation, new information was beginning to surface from the FBI and CIA.

CHAPTER 10:
Far Reaching Ramifications

When Ira Reiner fired the grand jury foreman and shut down the investigation, it closed the door on the last chance to determine the conspirators in Marilyn's death. The opportunity to acquire sworn testimony from all of the key witnesses still alive would never come again. In the months and years that followed, little or no activity was taking place on the Marilyn front.

During that time, with the help of my now adult sons, I began to assemble my memoirs. All of my information and notes were transferred to a device replacing my typewriter, called a personal computer.

Although new information was continuing to come out, many of my notes from the diary remained were unclear. Names like Iron Bob, Big Jim, and Eduardo still didn't have faces. Slowly I began to learn more.

During the mid 80's, the BBC produced a documentary about Marilyn Monroe. While watching, I saw an old film clip of President Achmad Sukarno of Indonesia getting off a plane. I remembered that Marilyn had made entries about him in her diary.

Marilyn wrote,

"Big Jim wanted me to do a job for them. They were trying to bring down a foreign leader who doesn't want to cooperate."

Jim O'Connell of the CIA's Far East Office contacted Marilyn about doing a series of sexy photos in Hollywood and at two New York hotels. In 1962, the Agency was actively trying to discredit Sukarno, as they believed there was a real danger that Indonesia would fall to the Communists.

The documentary stated that CIA documents revealed a scheme using Marilyn to discredit Sukarno. Knowing him to be a ladies' man, he was brought to Hollywood where an extravagant dinner and reception had been arranged and some movie stars invited.

Among those invited by the CIA was Marilyn Monroe. Her orders were to walk up to Sukarno, throw her arms around him and play the sexy dumb blonde. Marilyn had been carefully briefed and instructed to appear at the affair in a low cut dress. This went further than just Jim O'Connell asking her to do the Agency a favor. Briefing normally is reserved for individuals working on assignments or used in military terms. Debriefing, is passing on information to higher ups that operatives have obtained.

The director of the CIA at that time, John McCone, stated on public television in February, 1989, how all operatives were briefed and the extent to which the agency would go to influence or control foreign governments. McCone, who was handpicked to run the Central Intelligence Agency in 1961 by President John Kennedy, had restructured the organization since its Bay of Pigs fiasco in Cuba.

When I thought about it, she had also written in her diary about being approached by O'Connell and Maheu to do a sex film.

She wrote,

"Bob and Big Jim talked about shooting a film with Mr. Hughes to embarrass this diplomat."

It was not so far-fetched that the CIA would ask America's sex symbol to help them influence international politics. Maybe even discuss top secret information with her once they found out she was doing the same thing for the FBI.

Journalist Anthony Summers had reported a substantial effort was made to come up with a pornographic film, or at least some still photographs that could pass for Sukarno and a blond female engaged in sex. According to FBI records, when the available porno films failed to turn up an actor who could pass for Sukarno, the CIA strived to produce its own film. I discovered the outcome was a movie produced for the CIA by Howard Hughes, who had worked with Robert Maheu on other intelligence operations.

Reportedly Hughes actually delivered a film to O'Connell entitled "Happy Days," which starred a well-known Hollywood blond named Marilyn Monroe. The ultimate fate of the blackmail film was not reported, but a gallery owner recently found outtakes. We do know photo sessions between Marilyn and Sukarno did happen and there were eyewitness accounts of meetings in Hollywood and at a New York hotel.

Marilyn went to a higher calling when Jim O'Connell was promoted to Chief Regional Security officer for the entire Far East. He recruited Marilyn and Robert Maheu to assist him in his secret missions. The CIA's plan for the Far East was to have some leadership changes in Asia.

All of this strong attention to third World countries had been brewing for some time. Colonialism was coming to an end in Africa and Asia. Gandhi had got the British out of India, and the Dutch and French were next in Viet Nam. Most independent countries were forming new governments and looking for allies.

In 1955, at the invitation of President Sukarno, third world leaders agreed to gather in Bandung, Indonesia. American activist Paul Robeson was involved in the conference and Representative Adam Clayton Powell of New

York pleaded for the U.S. Government to attend. The CIA advised the President and Congress that the meeting was subversive because Indonesia was bringing together leaders of the decolonized peoples of Asia and Africa.

In 1961, Sukarno formed a political alliance called "The Initiative of Five". Malcolm X was a major contributor to this movement. It was later that CIA disclosures identified Robert Maheu in the attempted murder of Malcolm in Cairo, Egypt. Malcolm was there, meeting with Egyptian President Gamal Nasser regarding his appearance at the United Nations on the Human Rights issue. The American government was not ready for the subject of Human Rights.

February 11, 1962, Robert Kennedy arrived in Jakarta in a final attempt to prevent Indonesia from moving closer to the Communist bloc of nations. It is not known if Marilyn accompanied him, but we have reason to believe he had the sex film. What we do know is Sukarno was overthrown partly because of this scandal.

Marilyn attended communist meetings in Mexico after that episode. It is not confirmed, but suspected, that the CIA was behind this. Intelligence had been received that the Cubans were in negotiation with the Soviet Union regarding military support. This communist factor had followed Marilyn since the first pages of her diary. Was she an active government agent, communist party member, or just a showpiece on the world stage of international politics?

Almost certainly, the Kennedy White House was fully

aware and informed about Marilyn's activities with the CIA. If Marilyn didn't have a security clearance, why was she there? They were discussing national security matters that would affect the future of the world. If the Cubans and the Soviets joined forces, it could mean nuclear war.

So this is not just about Marilyn Monroe's unfortunate death, but her accounts relating to the inner workings of policy makers and bureaucrats. The people in this story had a great deal of power as representatives of the American People. It is important that history has a complete record of decisions and indiscretions made by these people. Because so many were employed by the government, they might have benefited from her timely death. Once you follow the paper trail, the list expands rather quickly.

Remember President Richard Nixon's Watergate? There is a distinct tie-in between Marilyn's relationship with the Fair Play For Cuba Committee and the CIA break in of the Democratic Headquarters to get or plant Cuban documents some 10 years later.

In an article entitled "Mission Impossible" by Eugenio Martinez, one of the Watergate burglars, and a Cuban, he stated,

"Cubans have never stopped fighting for the liberation of our country. I have personally carried out over 350 missions to Cuba for the CIA. I can't help seeing the whole Watergate affair as a repetition of the Bay of Pigs.

All of the agencies of the U.S. government were involved,

and they carried out their plans in so ill a manner that everyone landed in the hands of Castro - like a present. Generally, I talk to my CIA case officer at least twice a week and maybe on the phone another two times. I told him right away that Eduardo was back in town.

Eduardo was a name that all of us who had participated in the Bay of Pigs knew well. He had been the maximum representative of the Kennedy administration to our people in Miami. I then learned his name for the first time, E. Howard Hunt. We talked about the liberation of Cuba, and he assured us that the whole thing is not over and he blamed the Kennedy administration for not supporting us on the beaches of the Bay of Pigs."

When I started doing research for this project, the role of the United States Government in Marilyn Monroe's life was a glaring factor. I had come across the name Eduardo in Marilyn's diary and made a note, but didn't write down any specifics.

In her diary she wrote,

"The spy boys were really serious about killing Castro. Big Jim and Eduardo were actually involved in the Bay of Pigs..."

Marilyn was describing a meeting with Eduardo and Big Jim O'Connell, identifying them as being involved in the

Bay of Pigs. This entry was part of her extensive notes about her Kennedy meetings with the CIA.

Now we discover Eduardo to be the infamous Howard Hunt, of President Nixon's Watergate squad, involved in the Cuban campaign. Eugenio, if we opt to believe him, puts Hunt at the side of President Kennedy in 1961. Hunt was involved in the conspiracy plot to kill Castro in meetings with Jim O'Connell according to Marilyn. Eduardo was reportedly in Mexico at the same time as Marilyn and could have been with her in other activities such as the mysterious visit to the Cuban Embassy or Fair Play for Cuba Committee meetings.

I once asked Bob, after all his investigating, whom he thought killed Marilyn Monroe. He said most likely the Secret Service agents who were there or CIA under orders from Robert Kennedy. I guess my reaction was sort of revealing, because Bob went on to say,

"You think that's impossible? So was the Bay of Pigs, the assassination of John Kennedy, the assassination of Robert Kennedy, The disappearance of Jimmy Hoffa, the murder of Sam Giancana and the murder of Bernard Spindel. As a study of the unholy alliance between the Mafia and the CIA illustrates, Generals or Presidents don't ever have to pull the trigger. They just have to make the decision and live or die with it."

With that answer, there were now more suspects in Marilyn's death than in a 'Murder She Wrote' mystery. The growing list now includes the CIA, FBI, Secret Service, Mafia, Jimmy Hoffa, Dr. Greenson, Dr. Engelberg, Howard Hunt, Robert Maheu and the Kennedys.

Marilyn was trying to match wits with some very crafty individuals. I'm sure once she realized the situation she was in, suicide was an option unless she wanted to be water-boarded, have her fingernails pulled out one by one, or drugged into a senseless state.

CHAPTER 11:
The Marilyn Files

In 1991, William Speckin and Mel Bergman of Producer's Video contacted Bob Slatzer about producing a project based upon his "Marilyn Files" research. They wanted him do a video documentary, write a book, and produce the television version of our investigations. This was a fitting acknowledgement of our detective work, which we all felt provided the basis for a clear analysis of those last days in Marilyn Monroe's life.

Bergman and Speckin were determined to make the facts of Marilyn's death public. Their goal, according to them, was to re-open the case, lay out the facts surrounding the controversial death, and see justice done for Marilyn Monroe. It was a massive undertaking after 30 years, but Bob convinced me to go along. Besides, there was no compensation for appearances during all this time. At least these producers were willing to cover gas money.

When Bob finished his book, appropriately called "The Marilyn Files", I was impressed with the great detail that he went into. He gathered most of the people who were involved with the D.A. investigation and those he had talked to over the years and video taped them for the documentary.

This was kind of exciting because it offered me the rare opportunity to meet Jeanne Carmine and Terry Moore, two people I had read about in Marilyn's diary. Jeanne and Terry were completely convinced that Marilyn was murdered. Both had seen her diary and were aware of what she had written. That meant four of the people who had knowledge about the diary were there.

During the production, I spoke with her about some of the experiences we had both shared in this quest for Marilyn's justice. She told me it puzzled her why the statements she made were not released to the public, and she was here to fix that. When the subject of the diary came up, she seemed surprised by how much I knew, but by the time we finished chatting, both of us were sure we'd seen the same book.

While being taped, both Jeanne and Terry talked about the bad situation Marilyn found herself in and what they personally had seen or heard. Carmine mentioned that Marilyn believed her phones were being tapped and often would make her calls from pay phones. This not only collaborated what Bob had been saying about the wiretapping, but also verifies that Marilyn was connected to intelligence activities. How would she have known or even thought her phones were tapped?

Carmine and Moore also went into great detail about what she wrote in her diary, especially regarding her love affair with Bobby Kennedy. They talked about Marilyn and Bobby's secret trips to the beach and driving around the city in disguises, caught up in their whirlwind romance.

Both women described expressing to Marilyn their deep concern for her safety when she told them about the press conference she was planning. While talking to them, I also mentioned the entry Marilyn made in her diary regarding how they felt about Dr. Greenson.

She wrote,

"Dr. Greenson spent hours with me discussing world politics"

"Jeanne and Terry think he has some kind of control over me."

Although she didn't mention Greenson by name, Jeanne Carmine told me she always felt Marilyn was around too many psychiatrists, and they were making her extremely insecure. Carmine told me that despite her perceived image, that Marilyn was a tough woman particularly in the last years of her life.

I also had the opportunity to see someone for the first time in nearly thirty years, former Deputy District Attorney John Miner, who elaborated on the audiotapes of Marilyn, played for him by Dr. Greenson. Miner claimed that on these tapes Marilyn could be heard making plans for the future and obviously was not suicidal. He indicated that he filed two reports stating his opinion, one with the District Attorney's office and the other with the Coroner's Department. Miner told us that during the 1982 District Attorney Inquiry, investigators informed him that both of those reports had been lost.

This production was the largest gathering of people who knew something about Marilyn's death since the District Attorney Inquiry some ten years earlier. Others in attendance included my friend Jack Clemmons, Jim Hall, Milo Speriglio, Former Mayor of Los Angeles Sam Yorty, pathologists, forensic experts, friends of Marilyn, and of course Bob Slatzer.

During my interview, I casually told my story as I had done so many times before. It was difficult to believe that nearly thirty years had passed since that historic day in August, which changed my life forever. While telling my story, I didn't press the issue on the other revelations of the diary. No one seemed to want to talk about how deeply she was involved with the FBI or the Communist movement, and to tell the truth, neither did I.

By now, we all knew that many people had the motive and opportunity to murder Marilyn and that she hadn't committed suicide. The diary detailed how Marilyn was involved with each of these people, yet it was apparent that our legal system was not prepared to investigate the case based upon that or any other evidence we presented. Our hope with the documentary was to keep this story alive and not let this cover-up get buried with us.

The last person to be interviewed was a forensics pathologist named Dr. J. Dewitt Fox, who had studied Marilyn's case and determined that Marilyn could not have swallowed the amount of pills reported. No glass of water had been found at the crime scene and he said it would have been impossible to ingest them all without it. He also cited that in his experience as a forensics pathologist, one of the biggest red flags in her case was the fact that she had been discovered nude. Women who fall into her category of suicides almost never are found naked. That goes completely against the psychological profile of this type of case.

After his interview, I spoke with Dr. Fox about his analysis and how he thought Marilyn might have been killed. He told me that more than likely a suppository was used to administer the poison. He noted that if a more thorough autopsy had been performed and the organs not destroyed, it could have been easily determined.

Dr. Fox's logic made perfect sense, reminding me of a note I made about one of Marilyn's diary entries.

She wrote,

"They were discussing how to kill Castro. Johnny Roselli boasted about the Mafia's ability to infiltrate anybody's security to kill them. They have a pill to cram up Castro's butt."

This quote was relating to Marilyn's meeting with John Kennedy, the CIA, and members of the mafia. They were talking about using a suppository on Castro. This was the most revealing evidence I discovered during this production and fueled much of my research for years to come. Let's face it, the CIA and FBI were the ones best equipped to pull off a cover-up of this magnitude.

The documentary concluded that the Kennedys would have gained the most from Marilyn's death. She knew of some extremely sensitive political deals that could have handicapped the Kennedy Administration and perhaps ignited an international incident. Not to mention what she knew personally about John and Bobby Kennedy.

It was never my goal to determine who murdered Marilyn. I only wanted to establish her true cause of death. It appeared to me that if reasonable doubt could be established by this project, the investigation would stay alive. At the very least there would be grounds to continue the search for answers and one day close out the case of Marilyn Monroe.

For the television special, "The Marilyn Files Live," they brought together a panel of Prosecutors, Pathologists, and other experts from around the country to discuss whether there were enough contradictions to warrant a new grand jury investigation. The production was shot at Raleigh Studios in Hollywood complete with elaborate sets.

We created dramatic reenactments of scenes from Marilyn's house during the LAPD investigation, as recalled by Jack Clemmons, and the same for the Coroner's Office, as depicted by my accounts. It was the first time I was able to sit down and visualize that experience. We used actors to portray ourselves and recreate the circumstances to show the cover-up in vivid detail.

"The Marilyn Files Live" was broadcast internationally and hosted by actor Bill Bixby of "The Incredible Hulk" fame. The two-hour special aired prime time in over one hundred cities and was seen by millions worldwide. The audience response to the show was so huge that many cities re-ran our program the following week. The producers did a marvelous job of getting together a strong cast of people who either knew something about the case or who had a professional opinion on how it should have been handled.

Most of the people who were interviewed for the documentary, participated in the television special. We all hoped that public opinion would force officials to reconsider the suicide ruling. My thoughts were that this would be an excellent way of presenting the evidence to a new generation of people who were interested in Marilyn's death.

My interview with Bill Bixby was scheduled during the second hour of the live telecast. We went over the questions and I felt comfortable that the portrayal would be accurate. I was very surprised about how knowledgeable Bixby was about Marilyn's case. When we spoke backstage, he was very engaging and seemed genuinely captivated by our story.

What made this event so explosive was that it was being

broadcast live, worldwide. All eyes were on us and there were no re-takes or do-overs. Everybody was on the spot to tell the truth, as they knew it, and the public would be the judge as well as the jury. This was no place for the weak at heart, and the program didn't disappoint.

Bill Bixby did a masterful job of hosting the show and allowing each of us to present our experiences. The dramatic re-enactments scenes were powerful and really helped capture the essence of Jack's story and mine. Bixby asked us concise questions based on those scenes.

Even the former mayor of Los Angeles, Sam Yorty, who was supposed to supervise the City's investigation, explained what he was told by the Los Angeles Police Department. As Mayor during the time of Marilyn's death, he stated that LAPD Chief William Parker informed him that Bobby Kennedy was in Los Angeles the night of Marilyn's death. In fact, police officials knew he was staying at the Beverly-Wilshire Hotel.

Yorty also discussed how in the late sixties he requested a copy of the Los Angeles Police Department's files on Marilyn Monroe and was told none existed. Yorty went on to say he later discovered there probably was a file but his request was never fulfilled.

As the production went on there were subtle changes in the mood. The prosecutors, who were invited by the producers, began to get aggressive in their questioning. There had been no previous indication that any questions would be asked by anyone other than the moderators.

For instance, former Deputy District Attorney John Miner was placed in front of an impressive group of former District Attorneys and prosecutors from various States and Counties. They began to go into serious interrogation with Miner when he began discussing the audiotapes Dr. Greenson played for him. They asked Miner what was on the tape that had convinced him Marilyn had been murdered. He said he was not at liberty to disclose that information, but would testify if subpoenaed by grand jury.

They accused the former Deputy District Attorney of withholding evidence and said criminal charges should be filed for not answering their questions. Miner was so irritated by this line questioning that when he got up to leave the interview area, his microphone was still attached and he almost destroyed the set.

I wondered how the prosecutors had convinced Mel and Bill to change the script and allow them to threaten him with prosecution during the live broadcast. Maybe it was a District Attorney thing and their way to get back at Miner for not supporting the company line in his observations. I could certainly understand that, because it had also happened to Clemmons and me.

It was now apparent that all three of the public officials who were on duty at the time of Marilyn's death and said there was the possibility of homicide, had been vilified or discredited. Only John Miner, Jack Clemmons, and I were still willing and able tell our story about what had really happened in 1962. Neither Dr. Noguchi nor any other Police Officials would comment for the program.

Afterward everyone agreed that this was a complicated death provoking more questions than answers. In the end, we all laughed, shook hands and wondered how this tragedy could have happened. Most of the so-called experts would say this could never have happened if they had been the Coroner, District Attorney, Pathologist, Chief of Police or whatever capacity they represented.

I considered asking them if the White House, CIA, and FBI were advising them to keep their opinions to themselves how they would have reacted. They would have probably toed the lines just as many of these public officials did, because pressures within their departments undoubtedly demanded it.

Making money for appearances on television shows was never my aim or purpose. Exposing this Marilyn Monroe cover-up was a matter of principle, and selling my interview could be perceived as personal gain. No amount of money could ever make-up for what this Marilyn Monroe case had cost me, but discovering the truth might just help me to break even.

When the Marilyn File producers wanted me to sign a personal release form, Mel said they were going to sell this on DVD and would pay to use my interview. I should have known something was wrong. While writing my memoir, I was going through my mounds of paperwork and came across a check from Producer Video Inc. On it was stamped "in-sufficient funds". All I could say was, "So much for getting paid."

Anyway, this television production would be the last public outcry for the truth. The eyewitnesses to the cover-up and conspiracy surrounding the Marilyn Monroe death would never come together again.

Looking back in hindsight, the one element missing from "The Marilyn Files Live" television special was a recreation of the press conference Marilyn was planning. I often envisioned her in front of the press, reading what I had seen in the diary. She was probably the only one that had the charisma to tell the story and answer the questions. Did she see herself as a scorned woman looking for revenge, or as a disgruntled agent for the CIA and FBI, or just a party girl who felt used by powerful people? Like everything else that has happened since Norma Jean Baker became Marilyn Monroe, there was no answer.

Marilyn had always had to use her sexuality to exist. It was apparent to everyone who saw her that she was something special. She grew up in an unstable environment and according to her accounts, men had always offered her money, clothes, someplace to stay and promised to fulfill her many dreams since she was fifteen.

During her press conference, Marilyn may have told us how the FBI approached and requested her to perform certain assignments for "America." She might have elaborated on how a Hollywood actress was influenced with the promise of money, power, and success if she spied on somebody she knew.

According to Marilyn's diary, Roger Maheu recruited her to get information for the House Un American Activities Committee.

She wrote,

"The FBI wanted me to do something for America. They sent Iron Bob to ask me if Arthur was a Communist."

The FBI was actively gathering personal information on American citizens. They then discreetly leaked their version to groups such as the House Un-American Activities Committee, ardent anti-communists such as Sen. Joseph McCarthy, or police agencies who frequently used the unsubstantiated claims to destroy reputations or file false criminal charges. Marilyn was the perfect operative, and they offered to fulfill all of her dreams and more. However she didn't realize until it was too late, this path would dominate her destiny forever.

Marilyn might have also answered questions about how she was introduced to John Kennedy. It would be interesting to know exactly how this happened. Would she have said Robert Maheu arranged their meeting? In the clandestine world, "Iron Bob" was involved in some of the most notorious intelligence activities of the 20th century.

Maheu was the man who CIA officials thought of when they began entertaining the idea of killing Castro in 1960. His work for the Agency was primarily covert operations, from planning the assassination of foreign and domestic targets, to gathering information on American citizens. Maheu handled the jobs which intelligence agencies officially could not be involved with.

What would Marilyn have said about her meetings with CIA agent Big Jim O'Connell and mafia members like Johnny Roselli, who was contacted to set up a meeting with mob boss Sam Giancana to discuss killing Castro? According to her diary, Marilyn could have provided intimate details about the Governments association with the Mafia.

She may have told about the triangle, which was formed between the Mafia, CIA, and Kennedy Administration as they began planning the downfall of Castro. Marilyn heard much of the planning and, for better or worse, wrote it down in her diary.

After marriages to Arthur Miller and Joe DiMaggio ended in divorce, John and Robert Kennedy were the focal points of Marilyn's world right up until her final breaths. Her accounts may have included revealing details of her intimate relationship with the President of the United States, John F. Kennedy, who dumped her after his wife, Jackie Kennedy had found out about their relationship.

Without a doubt however, I believe Bobby Kennedy would have dominated Marilyn's press conference. According to most accounts, Bobby initiated his relationship with Marilyn to protect his brother's marriage. The President sent Bobby to explain why he could no longer see her, but he became attracted to Marilyn. They began a steamy affair that broke all the rules of national security and ultimately concluded with Marilyn's death.

These are details only Marilyn would have known and could have told if she had been allowed to hold her press conference. However, that was not the case and Marilyn took those secrets to the grave. The world as we know it today might have been just a little different, if she would have been able to speak.

CHAPTER 12:
My Investigation

When I first sat down to write this book, I wondered what the response would be. Although most of the people who shared this experience with me have died, I richly remember the passion they exhibited, telling a disbelieving society that Marilyn Monroe did not commit suicide. This project has provided me the opportunity to relive those experiences and recall some of my conversations with these people.

We had been recorded on many shows and given many interviews about Marilyn's case. A movie trailer was put on my website that featured statements from three of the investigators who were familiar with the circumstances surrounding her death.

One was a doctor who worked for the District Attorney's Office and was at her autopsy, another was the first Los Angeles Police officer at her house the night she died, and the third was me, who had signed her death certificate. Two others appearing on the trailer were friends of Monroe who had talked to her in the hours before she died.

Their statements repeated testimonies given to the Los Angeles County District Attorney's Office during its 1982 Inquiry. These five people represented the leading proponents for Marilyn's murder-not-suicide theory. I received this e-mail from an individual, who obviously was a huge Marilyn Monroe fan, and saw our movie trailer on YouTube.

Subject: Marilyn Project

FYI, you have MANY false facts in your trailer already. There are many supporters, like myself supporting and looking after Marilyn's GOOD NAME, whereby sensationalism for profits will not fly. Those days are LONG GONE.

So suggest you check your facts, sources et al, and make any literary or visual effort TRUE to Marilyn, or there is little choice but to call you out publicly via social networks, etc. which of course leads to POOR SALES...

Take your pick and good luck to you...

This is indicative of the confusion that has clouded the public's perception of the facts surrounding her death. I once had a well-known journalist from the BBC call me a liar before even asking me one question. Since my involvement, many conflicting stories about Marilyn's death have been written, which tends to clouds the truth. Disinformation has been this cover-up's most powerful weapon, and in today's socially driven information network, it's strong as ever.

Now let us profile this e-mailer. He or she was probably not even alive when Marilyn died. Even if they were, they probably were not privately informed about the facts of her death. Their knowledge was probably based upon her films and/or the stories written by journalists more confused than they were.

To call the public officials who saw the evidence that was available at that time not factual is absurd. If they are sincere about wanting to protect Marilyn's image, I would suggest they read this book to further understand how Marilyn's case evolved from beginning to end, and the implications of her death. I've been part of this investigation for too long and may have forgotten more about this case than 99% of the people will ever know. So a little thing like someone not believing my story cannot dissuade me.

My investigation of 'The Case of Marilyn Monroe' has continued to be an incredible but often-intense journey through Hollywood's biggest mystery. Even since shooting the Marilyn Files, new information and adventures have continued.

In 1993, I appeared on a special edition of "Hard Copy" called Marilyn Monroe: The Last Word. This television documentary was perhaps the most controversial program ever produced on the death of Marilyn Monroe. The show featured dramatic recreations of the love affair between Bobby Kennedy and Marilyn, along with many other aspects of her life. Paramount Pictures put up the money to produce this documentary, which obviously cost a pretty penny, but never received wide distribution. Rumors would later surface, stating that the Kennedy's influence scuttled the project.

On the program, journalist Anthony Summer's claimed Marilyn was fully aware of her actions with the CIA, and her role with the agency was no secret. He also stated Justice Department officals believed the Mafia murdered Marilyn Monroe in an attempt to smear the Kennedys, and said he was told by former FBI Assistant Director Courtney Evans to look in the direction of Sam Giancana. The documentary suggested the CIA was orchestrating this cloak of deception, which wasn't surprising at all.

Fred Otash, one of the men who wiretapped Marilyn's home, also appeared on the program. Otash made astonishing claims that Peter Lawford had contacted him the morning of Marilyn's death, frantic about what had happened that night. Lawford told him that Bobby Kennedy was there, and about the big fight. He wanted to hire Otash to help cover-up evidence at Marilyn's house.

If this statement was true, it meant that Peter Lawford had contacted the same private investigators that Jimmy Hoffa had hired to bug Marilyn's house. The same men who listened to wiretaps with Mafia gangsters hired by Sam Giancana.

Bob Slatzer, who appeared on the program as well, was as shocked as I was to hear these claims. But such goes the ongoing drama that has surrounded this infamous case. As I look back at my investigation and everything learned, I can't help but think how fate has played such a huge role in all this.

Let me begin with being at home with my family August 4, 1962. Little did I know that events were happening in West Los Angeles that would impact the rest of my life. Marilyn Monroe was dying and a cast of characters was there to make certain nobody would ever discover how.

Upon arriving to work that Sunday morning and discovering someone trying to remove Marilyn Monroe's body from the scene of a crime, things would never be the same. As far as the investigative aspect of this case, I have chronicled my recollection of the facts supported by evidence. No one from the Los Angeles County Coroner's Office has ever come forth publicly with a denial of anything I've ever said.

I'm sure that Dr. Curphey was not too happy with me because of my refusal to let it go. He probably would have told me, "Here's another fine mess you got the Coroner's Office into." There had been rumors through the grapevine saying he thought I was a traitor to our profession and to him. In his office, there was a big sign on the wall that said 'Silence is Golden'. I always thought it was referring to the noise, but now it seemed to be meant for the employees.

Being the last public official willing to talk about the Marilyn Monroe cover-up, let me start with what I saw at the Coroner's Office. That is where the basis for my investigation began, because I was forced to agree with an obviously flawed conclusion. Flawed because the investigation was incomplete and clearly rushed to the finish line.

First of all, there was no formal LAPD investigation report or even a preliminary report, which is required by law before closing any Coroner's case. The medical information from her doctors was not verified nor supported by the facts and toxicology reports further confused matters.

After seeing what my preliminary investigation had revealed, Dr. Curphey insisted none of it mattered. He ordered me to agree with his cause of death ruling that listed probable suicide and sign the certificate without many of the documents required. I wasn't Sherlock Holmes or even a veteran of thousands of Coroner's cases, but after three weeks of investigation it was apparent that something wasn't right and she actually died under a much more complicated set of circumstances.

District Attorney and Grand Jury Inquiries have been opened, and both closed their investigations after minimal to no inquiries into the true cause of death. Subsequent investigations by researchers such as Robert Slatzer, Donald Wolfe, Anthony Summers, and others have given us a broader timeline than even the District Attorney or the Los Angeles Police Department. These private investigations have used FBI and CIA disclosures and testimonies by ex-officials like me to discover the truth.

There are definite of links between the unfortunate murders of President John Kennedy, Senator Robert Kennedy, and Marilyn Monroe. The deaths or disappearances of many people involved in this case, has lead us to conclude something is missing. It is crystal clear that some individuals or agencies that were involved don't want the truth to be known. They have blocked all official Investigations, and anyone who didn't comply was discredited or worse.

Friends and family are left to figure out what happened. The Kennedys were a powerful family with money and influence. Perhaps they were able to discover the facts surrounding the deaths of their love ones despite the cover-up. Marilyn Monroe had no known relatives, and in her case, the conspirators probably thought they could keep everyone quiet, and thus leaving the American public to draw its own conclusion.

Every step was taken in order to make the cover up work. The FBI gobbled up evidence, the CIA paid journalist to hide their involvement, and the Kennedy White House blocked all other media coverage. From the first hours of this assignment, the people at Marilyn's house made a strong attempt to report inaccurate information, and it has been almost impossible to sort out the truth.

The hard evidence supports that Marilyn Monroe died either by accidental overdose or was assassinated by a person or persons unknown. If you want to know why other public officials didn't concur, then you need to understand these people had jobs and yielded to the intense pressure, precipitating the highly sophisticated cover-up that followed.

For instance, Marilyn's body was discovered by her housekeeper, Eunice Murray, a supposed nurse assigned to Marilyn's care by her psychiatrist, Dr. Ralph Greenson. Some evidence suggests that as many as seven hours may have elapsed before the authorities were called, the night Marilyn died. Credible sources have stated her body was taken to a hospital during the interim, and later returned to the house.

Walter Schaefer, owner of the Schaefer Ambulance Service, was recorded saying an ambulance was dispatched to Marilyn's home. He claimed his company's paramedics transported her to Santa Monica Hospital, and then returned her body to the house, placing it in her bedroom. Evidence also points to several additional people present at Marilyn's home during that time.

Bob told me he spoke with Inez Melson, Marilyn's business manager, and she stated that four representatives from 20th Century Fox were present during those early morning hours. Melson claimed the studio personnel were removing anything that could tarnish Marilyn's reputation.

The most compelling part of my investigation has been the journal or diary allegedly written by Marilyn Monroe. In her own words, she wrote the accounts of the last seven or eight years of her life. This book disappeared from the safe at the Los Angeles County Coroner's Office two days after it was brought in. Maybe County or Government officials removed the book to take it out of circulation, or maybe the motive was all about money. We may never know.

My investigation shows that around 7:00pm on Saturday night, August 3, Robert Kennedy, Peter Lawford, and two Secret Service Agents came to visit Marilyn. Kennedy was adamant about finding the book. On the wire tapper's audiotape, heard by Bob Slatzer, he described a fight that turned violent. Slatzer heard Peter Lawford saying,

"Marilyn, Marilyn, give him what he wants."

She started screaming, and Bob heard what sounded like a loud slap and someone falling. Peter then told Robert Kennedy,

"We better get out of here. Someone might have heard this commotion."

Slatzer heard the door slam and Marilyn crying in the background. He thought Bobby said, "Give her something to calm her down." Even though it sounded off mike and muffled, he was inclined to believe that's what was said.

Peter Lawford and Bobby Kennedy left Marilyn's house about 8 PM and Lawford apparently took him to the airport. There are witnesses who claim to have talked to her between 8:00 and 10:30 PM. Jeanne Carmine told me that Marilyn called her at 10:00pm that night, asking her to come over. Claiming exhaustion, Carmine declined, but noticed something "strange" in Marilyn's voice.

Marilyn was obviously alive when Kennedy left the house. I know this, because she wrote about the night events in her diary. So what else happened to Marilyn that night? Did the Secret Service give her a lethal dose of sedative, as Bob believed?

What about Sam Giancana's three hit men? Did they find their way into Marilyn's house and slip her a suppository. You can't eliminate the CIA and their hit man Robert Maheu either.   In fact, any government agency, including the United States Army, is not above suspicion, because of the sensitive information Marilyn could have known.

According to wiretaps, Peter Lawford arrived back at the house some point during the night, after Marilyn died. Fred Otash, one of the wire tappers, claimed Lawford was searching for the diary and love letters. It was here that the cover-up began as they tried to figure out how to report the death to the police and Coroner.

According to Lawford's ex-wife, he said that the Kennedys assured everyone involved that there would be no proper inquiry into her death. First, Lawford, the Doctors, and the housekeeper concocted a reasonable story so no real investigation would take place. Then they had to convince the police that this was a simple suicide, and get the Coroner to release the body to a friendly mortuary that Fox studio had contacted. That turned out to be Westwood Mortuary. All was going well until, as Dr. Curphey put it, I got my hands on it.

After the attempt to remove Marilyn's body to an outside mortuary failed, her remains were brought to the Hall of Justice for a formal investigation. The Los Angeles County Coroner did a good job of helping confuse the facts. There were at least two people at the autopsy, Dr. Noguchi and John Miner. I was told as many as five were at the procedure, but couldn't confirm these reports or identify whom they were.

Dr. Curphey's toxicologist Dr. Ralph Abernathy had found no poison in the blood when he first test Marilyn's body. Later, he reported finding enough poison to kill five people, with no determination how the poison was administered. He then destroyed her organs under orders from Dr. Curphey, preventing any future test from being made. According to County records, there is only two times in the history of Los Angeles that the liver or any other tissue sample was lost: Marilyn Monroe and Robert Kennedy. This is important to note.

The Suicide Investigation Team report determined in all probability Marilyn took her own life. There was some controversy as to how she did it, but no effort was made to solve this glaring mystery. Dr. Curphey impaneled two doctors that were supposed to make a thorough investigation, but all of their conclusions were based on statements from Marilyn's doctors and published news accounts.

No report was ever made to the Coroner's Medical

Department identifying who prescribed the many medication containers found at the scene. Dr. Engelberg told the Coroner and the police that he had prescribed the Nembutal tablets found in Marilyn's throat along with other medications. However, none of those other medications were found in Marilyn's system or those from the empty containers. Furthermore, no container or prescription was ever found for the Chloral Hydrate.

According to Dr. Curphey and Suicide Team Investigators, Doctor Greenson testified as to how the death occurred and Marilyn's state of mind. However, only a week after her death, Dr. Greenson stated he never believed Marilyn's death was suicide. During an interview with Deputy District Attorney John Miner, the doctor expressed his true opinion and played audiotapes of Marilyn's most recent conversations to prove it.

The Los Angeles Police Department did a better job of hiding the facts. There were at least three separate reports by LAPD officers to determine how and when she died. High-level detectives were assigned to determine the facts surrounding her death, yet almost none of their official reports or any dialog with the Coroner or Suicide Team, remain in LAPD files.

Los Angeles Police Department Chief of Police, William Parker, supervised the official investigation. According to published reports, Parker assigned Captain James Hamilton to Marilyn's case, who handled the main investigation in an atmosphere of secrecy that excluded even his most trusted employees. Hamilton was a friend of Bobby Kennedy, having worked with him years earlier. According to Jay Margolis in his book, "Marilyn Monroe: A Case for Murder" Hamilton may have been a source of intelligence within the LAPD for Kennedy.

Public funds provide the Police, Coroner, and the District Attorney with a decent budget to investigate unusual deaths in the City and County of Los Angeles. For the most part, they do an excellent job under difficult situations. In this case, most likely, they were met with the highest power that Federal Agencies have over local municipalities, besides jurisdiction, "National Security." This classification is a way of protecting government interests and discouraging all local inquiries.

After apparently running into these kinds of complications, no official LAPD report was made for the Coroner's Office that contained all the facts. I may be getting a little ahead of myself, because LAPD might have given the report to Dr. Curphey and he personally chose to hide it. All I know is that in 1962, all official inquiries died suddenly.

Needless to say, after the official Corner's case was closed, a flood of information continued to arise, suggesting a cover-up. Marilyn Monroe's phone records from early August until her death went missing from the phone company. Bob Slatzer once told me that only two entities had enough power to seize phone records without a court order, J. Edgar Hoover of the FBI and the Kennedy Administration.

By 1993, my knowledge of Marilyn's case may have been second to only Bob Slatzer, who was my investigative partner. Our combined experiences had brought television and news media from around the world to hear us discuss the case. My participation with two District Attorney investigations and a short-lived grand jury probe has provided me insight into Marilyn's death unlike any others. In the next few chapters, I will attempt to quickly tie together all I have learned.

CHAPTER 13:
From the Pens of Researchers

In the 50 years following Marilyn Monroe's death, there has been intense speculation by many armchair sleuths and journalists as to whether Marilyn took her own life. All the participants have been named and sinister plots investigated, with every imaginable scenario being described despite the massive cover-up. To close this little piece of history, we'll look at some of the other significant investigations into Marilyn's death.

Internationally recognized private investigator and director of the Nick Harris Detective Agency, Milo Speriglio, wrote a book entitled "Crypt 33: The Saga of Marilyn Monroe." In this book, he accused President John Kennedy of ordering the hit. According to Speriglio, Monroe was the victim of a national security management hit by the CIA and the Mob.

He stated the motive to be Marilyn becoming a threat to the family. Calling the White House almost everyday, Marilyn became a hot topic among Washington insiders. After announcing a press conference with the threat of blowing the lid off her relationship with the brothers, she had become a security risk.

Speriglio describes how Johnny Roselli, known for his attempted assassination of Fidel Castro and allegedly Robert Kennedy, arrived at Marilyn's house with two associates. He says they overpowered her and forcefully administered a killer enema. His assertion was that Joe Kennedy, the President's father, hired Sam Giancana to kill Marilyn, and Giancana and Hoffa had set Bobby up for a scandal. However, the Kennedy cover-up worked when Peter Lawford sped Bobby away from the house and they avoided a family disaster.

Most of his conclusions were based on the tapes that Bernard Spindel and Fred Otash had recorded. I knew Milo and although we didn't get along, his research was respected. Bob once told me that Otash was offering his tapes to the highest bidder, so the possibility existed Milo heard the recordings. It would have been nice if District Attorney officials would have bought these tapes and made them public, but just like everything else, they probably would have simply disappeared forever.

The rectal insertion was my hot choice for cause of death, because of the lack of barbiturates in her stomach. When Doctor Abernathy, the County Toxicologist, destroyed the organs, it prevented any further test for a suppository. Marilyn wrote in her diary about the CIA providing Roselli with a pill or poison to kill Castro, so maybe Milo was on the right track.

"Goddess" author, Anthony Summers, television producer for the BBC, turned up evidence of the Robert Maheu and Howard Hughes, Monroe film in his investigation. His CIA disclosures verified Marilyn's description of being approached by Jim O'Connell and Maheu with a plan to discredit the Indonesian President.

Summers wrote that Marilyn did not intentionally kill herself, and left open the possibility of murder. His research indicated that Bobby Kennedy was in the house that night and found Marilyn already drugged. He then called an ambulance to take her to the hospital, but she died. Evidence of him being at the house was destroyed by Peter Lawford to avoid his association with the death.

In a later revelation, Summers quoted an unnamed source, who claimed to have heard tapes of Marilyn's final night. The source said Bobby and Marilyn were screaming at each other while Peter Lawford was trying to calm them down. At one point, according to the informant, there were sounds of a struggle, and Robert Kennedy may have pushed Marilyn onto the bed. He also said the tapes sounded like they were edited. The tapes, according to Summers, left the impression that Marilyn was dead when Bobby left the house.

Writing about the assassination of John F. Kennedy, he rejected the findings of the Warren Commission, and claimed that Kennedy was killed by a right-wing conspiracy, possibly including major organized crime figures, such as Johnny Roselli, Carlos Marcello, Santo Trafficante, and Sam Giancana. Other figures possibly involved included David Ferrie, Gerry Patrick Hemming, Guy Banister, and E. Howard Hunt.

I have to give Summers credit for his persistence in finding out what happened to Marilyn Monroe. At first, we disagreed on what happened in the Coroner's Office, but he was the first to uncover CIA documents that confirmed what was in her diary. The disclosures stated that Marilyn had worked with the CIA to discredit a foreign diplomat, something I had told County Officials many years earlier.

In the book entitled "Double Cross," written by Sam & Chuck Giancana, nephew and brother of Sam Giancana respectively, it is stated that Marilyn's killers listened to wiretaps and waited for an opportune time to strike. When the hit men overheard the argument between Marilyn and Bobby, it provided an opportunity to execute their murder; Kennedy had ordered Marilyn sedated, and left the house. Later, the assassins sneaked into her bedroom and gave her a lethal suppository.

This book supported the theory that Sam Giancana and the Mafia were involved in the murder. Marilyn said she first saw Giancana in New York at a meeting with the CIA. Fast forward to the ill-fated weekend party that Frank Sinatra gave, this is where the mob decided to make their move. Hoffa would provide the wire tapers and Giancana the muscle.

Was Marilyn really murdered this way? I'm not sure. What I can say is that what happened during those recording sessions with Bernard Spindel and Fred Otash made a lot of people think that Sam Giancana had the Hollywood actress killed.

"The Last Days of Marilyn Monroe" by Donald Wolfe is based on interviews that reveal much of the same information that I have. Wolfe adds his own extensive inquiry to those of several other journalists, based on interviews that have revealed a more candid telling with the passage of time.

His evidence seems clear and convincing that there was a murder. By the time of her death, Marilyn Monroe was so enmeshed in sex, highest-level politics, the Mafia, and concerns over national security that her life was in the gravest danger.

In his investigation, he discovered that she had maintained a long-standing sexual relationship with both John F. Kennedy and Robert Kennedy, and had a diary that included the content of many sensitive conversations with them concerning things like Castro and the Mafia. His chronicles of her final days names the killer, documents the mode of death, and identifies those who orchestrated the cover-up.

Donald Wolfe, who was an acquaintance of Marilyn's and a long-time screenwriter, investigated the facts surrounding Marilyn's death. His indignation that the death processing was not followed accordingly with proper legal procedures, such as a coroner's inquest and a grand jury investigation, were the same as mine.

My investigative partner and good friend, Robert Slatzer was a screenwriter and author. He published two books on Marilyn, "The Life and Curious Death of Marilyn Monroe" in 1974 and "The Marilyn Files" in 1993. Bob, who shared a very special relationship with Marilyn, was a leading authority on the subject and was among the first researchers to proclaim that she did not commit suicide.

From my point of view, Robert Slatzer assembled the largest body of evidence on Marilyn's death, including gathering officials from the Coroner's Office, District Attorney's Office, and Los Angeles Police Department, whom all proclaimed suicide was not the cause.

Bob was the first journalist to uncover the infamous wiretap recordings and make the public aware of their existence. The most significant evidence of a crime stems from these audiotapes, which Jimmy Hoffa had recorded. Bob heard some of these tapes and told me there was no telling how many different edited versions there were in existence.

Bob believed that Marilyn's diary was the motive for her murder, and the wire-tapping's had provided him the proof. He heard those recordings and was hopeful that one day they would resurface. Bob's exhaustive investigation into

Marilyn's death has uncovered many other details, which never may have been exposed without his research.

From my perspective, the wiretaps and Marilyn's diary provided all the evidence needed to discount the suicide theory. Johnny Roselli and Sam Giancana said that the CIA had provided them with every imaginable kind of pill to kill someone. Many of which were not detectable with normal tests. All of this, combined with my experiences at the Coroner's Office, leaves very little doubt about her death.

This suicide thing had bothered me from the start. If you have been following the evidence, then one could make an argument that she had gotten in a little over her head, and decided to end it all, or had accidentally taken too many pills while trying to go to sleep. However, the facts do not lead to these conclusions, and all of this is not just another conspiracy theory.

I go back to the first report that came out of the toxicology lab. Thirty Nembutal tablets lodged in the throat and no trace of anything that could have killed her in the stomach or blood. This was the first evidence that should have raised a red flag. There wasn't even a trace of any other prescribed medications that she was supposed to be legitimately taking. Even with all those prescription bottles sitting on her bedside nightstand, none were present inside her system.

The death certificate stated 'Acute Barbiturate Poisoning' due to 'Ingestion of Overdose'. A final copy of the toxicology report revealed '4.5 milligrams per cent' of Barbiturates in the blood and '8.0 milligrams per cent' of Chloral Hydrate. Where did this poison come from? Dr. Engelberg stated he had prescribed the Nembutal capsules that Dr. Noguchi said killed her. No one came forward with a prescription for Chloral hydrate. This is a sedative used in the short-term treatment of insomnia and induces sleep before surgery. It comes as a capsule and liquid form, either orally ingested or utilized as a suppository to insert rectally.

Since numerous capsules and containers of prescription drugs were found at the scene, all orally taken, it is difficult to conceive that some trace of these drugs would not be found in the stomach or intestinal tract. Since there are no findings of these drugs in the stomach, and knowing the results of the toxicology, one must seriously consider the possibility of an injection or the use of a suppository to account for the toxicology findings.

The question of the Nembutal is still a mystery. How did these pills get in her throat, and did they kill her? There are 3 possibilities:

1. She failed in her attempt to commit suicide when they lodged in her throat.
2. She took them to go to sleep or for pain either on purpose or accidentally.
3. Someone crammed them in her mouth to make it look like suicide.

No answers would have been forthcoming if the body

had been taken to Westwood mortuary. The Coroner's Office would have assigned a Deputy Coroner to go to the mortuary and evaluate the case. Our doctor may or may not have decided to perform an autopsy. He could have chose to go along with the police assessment of the facts and just take blood samples. Fox Studio, who had called the mortuary, could have influenced this decision.

Either way, this would have added an extra day to the process, allowing the capsules to dissolve into the bloodstream before they could be discovered in the throat. No doubt that when I called for the body to be brought downtown, this forced a change of plans.

What this case always needed was someone to supervise the investigation and guarantee that the facts would be known. However, with the District Attorney's Office involved in the initial cover-up, all outside attempts to investigate her death have been thwarted in ways that can only make you scratch your head. Even the Los Angeles County Grand Jury could not penetrate the web of deceit and cover-up surrounding this case.

Future journalist and researchers must continue trying to solve the mystery surrounding Marilyn's death. Their writings are the impetus that keeps this story alive and provides the best opportunity for a new investigation to uncover the truth. The only advice I would offer is to begin with the U.S. Government and it's Intelligence agencies.

CHAPTER 14:
The FBI, CIA, and Mafia

Marilyn's involvement with U.S. Intelligence and Organized Crime is perhaps the most curious aspect of this investigation. Her association with these entities seems almost impossible to conceive, but the weight of evidence, which includes FBI and CIA disclosures, is indesputable.

Marilyn's own words may have offered the best description of her situation. The activities detailed in her diary reflected a woman trapped in world with no escape. The public knew her Hollywood image, but beneath it was a complicated reality involving matters shaping the future of America. Once Marilyn got in, there was no getting out, and even her Hollywood fame couldn't save her. She was a little fish in a big pond, and we all know how that story ended.

Let's take a deeper examination of roles played by the FBI, CIA, and Mafia in Marilyn Monroe's death.

The Federal Bureau of Investigations is the nation's oldest and most prestigious intelligence agency. For many years, they were America's protectors, and the public loved them. J. Edgar Hoover was the top watchdog and wielded the power to do whatever deemed necessary for preserving public security. However, there was a fine line between security and violating the constitution. At some point, Hoover began to cross it.

A prime illustration was the Bureau illegally spying on members of the civil rights movement. The treatment of Martin Luther King Jr. and actress Jean Seberg are two cited examples.

Hoover directed the FBI to track King in 1957 and concluded that King was dangerous due to communist infiltration. After accusing one of King's most trusted advisers of working as an agent of communist influence over the movement, he placed wiretaps on King's home and office phones and bugged King's rooms in hotels as he traveled across the country. King was the victim of FBI leaks of unverified information to his bank, insurance company and organization. The agency even sent taped conversations with other women to his wife. King was assassinated with more than one FBI agent at the scene in Memphis.

Seberg, an actress from Iowa, was also targeted by Hoover. He leaked false stories, claiming she was pregnant by a member of the Black Panther Party, whose cause she supported. The backlash of this smear campaign caused Seberg a series of nervous breakdowns that eventually killed her. The police report stated that she massively overdosed on barbiturates, and "probable suicide" was ultimately ruled the official cause of death by the French Coroner.

J. Edgar Hoover's tactics for protecting America from the

so-called Communist threat knew no bounds and when Arthur Miller's name landed on his list, he catalogued every person Miller associated with. Marilyn's name surfaced at that time. She was recruited to retrieve information on Arthur Miller, detailing his Communist activities.

The FBI connection with Marilyn Monroe began from that moment, and ended with bugging her house for the final six months of her life. Evidence suggests that FBI Director Hoover had shown his interest in her activities for many years. He reportedly spent hundreds of hours listening to tapes taken from every room in her house, or any house and any hotel she stayed at. We can assume that the Federal Bureau of Investigation was well aware of Marilyn's involvement with White House affairs, and knew from taped conversations she had began documenting her activities. Hoover was obviously concerned that anything Monroe passed on about the President or U.S. Intelligence would pose a tremendous threat to National Security.

When Marilyn went to Mexico City in 1962, she had meetings with assembled communist activists. FBI and CIA disclosures have also placed Lee Harvey Oswald there that same year. Is it possible that Marilyn Monroe attended a meeting with Oswald in 1962? Little more than a year before he allegedly assassinated President Kennedy? What we do know is that after her trip, the FBI director in Mexico City sent a memo to Hoover about Marilyn attending the "Fair Play For Cuba "Meetings.

The FBI's primary focus seemed to be with domestic communist activities. Government documents indicate they were very much aware of Marilyn being in Mexico City in 1962, and that those FBI officials in Mexico filed a report on visits to the Soviet and Cuban embassies. According to J. Edgar Hoover's secretary, two weeks after this report reached FBI headquarters, Hoover went to the White House to talk to President Kennedy about her involvement with the Cubans.

At least in part, his purpose was not only warning Kennedy about the national security implications, but also to rub the President's womanizing in his face. Nothing in the available record shows what was discussed at that meeting, or if Hoover mentioned Monroe's involvement with the FBI or CIA endeavors. Once you start to include international issues into this conversation, it broadens the scope of people who could have serious concerns.

Let's get this straight; the closest the world has come to nuclear war was the Cuban Missile Crisis of October 1962, which was only two months after Marilyn died. Fidel Castro, afraid of an assassination by the CIA and an invasion by the United States, had negotiated with the Soviet Union to install nuclear missiles to protect Cuba. The planning and construction of those weapons was occurring simultaneously with the "Fair Play For Cuba" meetings.

It's hard to believe that the possibility of this kind of activity was not being discussed at the White House. Marilyn was at the CIA meetings, where the threat of Castro was being talked about. She was in Mexico City with the Fair Play for Cuba Committee when the missile bases were being armed.

The Cuban populace easily noticed the arrival and deployment of the missiles and hundreds of reports reached U.S. Intelligence. Countless sightings of large trucks traveling through towns were being discussed in the circles that Marilyn was traveling in. These trucks were reportedly carrying the launchers to the bases.

Finally, we don't know what Marilyn learned about the Cuban missiles or any other clandestine activities, but we do know that Hoover began wiretapping Marilyn's home and was informed about all calls received and dialed in her house regarding any potential national security matters.

With the Cuban missile situation in the deployment stage and the CIA directing secret missions in Cuba, anything Marilyn said on the subject, in her house, or on her phone, would have been of interest to the Cubans, Soviets, and the rest of the world for that matter.

The Bureau wanted to know everything about Marilyn, the CIA, the Kennedys, and all national security issues being discussed. They monitored her activities around the clock, so it stands to reason that Hoover knew key details about her death. The question we have to ask is why this information was withheld from the public. Did J. Edgar Hoover and the Federal Bureau of Investigation consider Marilyn's death a matter of national security?

When the wiretaps revealed that Marilyn had written notes on Bobby Kennedy's conversations and details about some CIA meetings, they probably went on high alert. The FBI always fought an all out war against crime, subversion, and communism. So their presence kind of makes sense, considering the history between the Marilyn and them.

Marilyn's fate will always be tied to the FBI and Robert Maheu, in my opinion. From his first contact with her, they formed a relationship that may have been more strategic than even her relationships with the Kennedys. Perhaps someday, the Bureau will release more information on their interactions before and after Arthur Miller. Somehow I believe that Monroe and Maheu had ties deeper than we may ever know.

Now let's examine her circumstances with the CIA. The first time the Central Intelligence Agency was mentioned by Marilyn is when she met Jim O'Connell. In her diary, this occurred at a meeting in New York with President John Kennedy and his advisors. She called him Big Jim of the Spy Boys. O'Connell, at that time, was Coordinator of the Assassination Plots against Castro for the CIA.

According to the diary and Senate Hearing disclosures, Marilyn Monroe was meeting with John Kennedy, then President of the United States; Jim O'Connell, Central Intelligence Agency Coordinator; Robert Maheu, FBI and CIA operative; and Mafia members Sam Giancana and

Johnny Roselli, all discussing illegal things like killing somebody.

Marilyn's work for the Central Intelligence Agency didn't end there. In 1962, Jim O'Connell was transferred to Asia, where he became Chief Regional Security Officer for the Far East. This job included numerous attempts to undermine foreign governments or assassinate their leaders. Marilyn would make entries in her diary about working with O'Connell and Robert Maheu, planning the overthrow of a government. CIA disclosures have confirmed her description of those meetings and the events she wrote about in her diary.

After Marilyn met John Kennedy, he was elected to President of the United States and shortly thereafter, as described in her diary, she began attending high-level intelligence meetings. This chain of events leaves little doubt that Marilyn was well on her way to becoming an agent for the United States Government.

CIA operatives are certainly not above suspicion in Marilyn's death. Surely after hearing about how unstable her home life had become, they worried about her knowledge of agency affairs. Central Intelligence was involved in the assassination of World Leaders from its inception, according to its own disclosures. Still, there wasn't a lot of information on their activities concerning the matter. The agency was able to restrict newspapers from reporting about certain events. For example, the CIA's plots to overthrow the governments of Iran in 1953 and Guatemala in 1954 were not reported by most news organizations.

Even before the Bay of Pigs, CIA minds were strategizing to keep Cuba out of Communist hands. Their attempt to use the Mafia to help overthrow Castro began during the Eisenhower administration. This meant that O'Connell's plot to kill the Cuban leader started before John Kennedy took office. This of course was illegal, not that the Mafia cared, but the House Select Committee on Assassinations did call the CIA into question. Under sworn testimony, Big Jim O'Connell answered these questions from the committee:

Question: *(Committee)* When did this operation begin? In other words, when did you first meet with Roselli?

Answer: *(O'Connell)* That would have been September of 1960.

Question: *(Committee)* And who was present during this conversation? This is the one at the Plaza Hotel in New York.

Answer: *(O'Connell)* Maheu, Roselli, and myself.

Question: *(Committee)* Did there come a time when other individuals were brought into the project?

Answer: *(O'Connell)* At this point in time, no.

Question: *(Committee)* When, if fact, did other individuals become involved in the operation?

Answer: *(O'Connell)*   Well, after Mr. Roselli rather reluctantly agreed to participate in this type of operation, he brought in other individuals who I knew only by pseudonyms, "Sam Gold" and "Joe One Joe."

Question: *(Committee)* When these individuals were identified using these names had you met them personally?

Answer: *(O'Connell)*   No.

Question: *(Committee)* When did you first learn their true identities? The identities of Sam Gold and Joe.

Answer: *(O'Connell)*   In the Sunday paper, there was an article, identifying the leaders of the Mafia. In that article there were pictures of Sam Gold, who was identified as Momo Giancana and Joe, was identified as Santos Trafficante. And Mr. Maheu claimed this was the first time he was aware of just who we were dealing with.

Question: *(Committee)* Alright, what did you do upon learning that the individuals involved in this operation were in fact organized crime leaders?

Answer: *(O'Connell)*   I contacted Colonel Edwards and told him what we had discovered, or at least, as far as I was concerned, it was the first indication I had who we were dealing with, and appraised them of his identities.

Question: *(Committee)*   And what did he say to you? What instructions did he give you, if any?

Answer: *(O'Connell)*   Well, he just said, well this is probably what we could have expected, I suppose. And I don't want to be quoting him, because I don't recall really what he said, but apparently he did not feel we should alter our approach to the assignment.

Question: *(Committee)*   Did he give you any further instructions -- any additional instructions -- upon learning the identities of these persons?

Answer: *(O'Connell)*   No. As I recall we just proceeded.

These meetings took place prior to John Kennedy's election, headed up by Vice President Richard Nixon. After Kennedy became President, he took charge of the plot and participated in these planning sessions with the assassins.

When I read Marilyn's account of some of the meetings with these people in 1962, it didn't have the same meaning that it does now. There was more information in that book, but I didn't have the time or inclination to digest it.

Bits and pieces of information have been released through the Freedom Of Information Act that has made me more knowledgeable about the importance of the contents. The FBI and CIA documents, and what other researchers were uncovering, brought her words to life. This has been a slow process, but the scenario that many denied is coming into full view. At first, everyone thought I was crazy, but time has proved Lionel Grandison to be correct.

A CIA document appeared sometime in the early 1990's, regarding the transcripts of wiretaps on Marilyn's house. A researcher had gone to the CIA's Agency Release Panel with a request, under the Freedom of Information Act, to release existing documents their possession regarding government wiretaps on Marilyn Monroe's telephones.

In the 3rd of August, 1962, CIA report, written only a day before Marilyn Monroe's death, reveals why some high government officials were in a state of extreme anxiety. The Kennedy brothers had been imparting sensitive information to Marilyn, and she was writing a lot of it down in her little red "diary of secrets."

CIA wiretaps of conversations between Marilyn Monroe and Robert Kennedy revealed some interesting points. The report contained these statements:

1. Subject repeatedly called the Attorney General and complained about the way she was being ignored by the President and his brother.
2. Subject threatened to hold a press conference and would tell all.
3. Subject made reference to "bases" in Cuba and knew of the President's plan to kill Castro.
4. Subject made reference to her "diary of secrets" and what the newspapers would do with such disclosures.

A part of the report is blacked out for National Security reasons, and the document is signed JAMES ANGLETON, who at the time was the Chief of Counterintelligence for the CIA.

During the early 1960's, the Nuclear Arms Race was in full effect. Russia and the United States were playing a dangerous game of chicken by testing nuclear weapons at an alarming rate. On July 17, 1962, Robert Kennedy, with presidential adviser General Maxwell D. Taylor at his side, witnessed one of these nuclear tests, code named "Little Feller", and was fully briefed on U.S. Military nuclear capabilities. Any widespread discussion would have brought United States Military Intelligence into the picture.

The CIA's bugging of Marilyn's house has deep implications. They were monitoring all conversations Bobby would have had with the White House or any other individuals discussing sensitive security issues. Most importantly, CIA operatives heard everything happening before, during, and after Marilyn's death. They knew what transpired that night, and how the investigation progressed during the day. The agency knew every detail about Marilyn Monroe, and when they left didn't even bother to take their equipment.

After reading the disclosure, I wished that the grand jury could have seen the same document. Maybe that would have turned the tides and forced the District Attorney's Office to continue their so-called threshold Inquiry until they got it right. If they just could have determined what killed her, then we would have been a step closer.

Although they could not find her diary, they knew it had been in the Coroner's Office. It was apparent that the Coroner had been forced to cover up the cause of death. Maybe the CIA or the FBI had asked them to help conceal what actually happened, just as they had done with the Los Angeles Police Department. Probably The District Attorney was plausibly in a no win situation.

The significance of the wiretap disclosure has to do with the fact that Monroe was murdered the following day. Any suggestion that somehow the CIA was involved in a domestic murder of an American citizen is not too far-fetched when considering past abuses from the agency's Counter Intelligence program, with its "absolute security at any cost" philosophy.

Whether or not the CIA authorized the hit is unknown, but the way her body was found and moved around, the fashion of which reports were changed to reflect suicide, and the theft of her secret diary less than 48 hours after it arrived at the Coroner's Office all have similarities to covert CIA methods used to conceal the truth.

In 1960, Retired US Army Colonel Truman Smith, writing in *Reader's Digest* about the KGB, who were the Soviet's version of the CIA, declared:

"It is difficult for most of us to appreciate its menace, as its methods are so debased as to be all but beyond the comprehension of any normal person with a sense of right and wrong."

One of the KGB methods that the good colonel found so despicable was the making of sex films to be used as blackmail. He wrote,

"People depraved enough to employ such methods, find nothing distasteful in more violent methods."

We would like to think that our own Intelligence Agency would heed this set of values, but as we found out in Iraq, no rules are observed when it comes to protecting America. During the time of Colonel Smith's statement, Jim O'Connell began to use Marilyn to devise his own plan. After seeing her at the Castro plot meetings, he thought her perfect for his plans in the Far East.

I assume O'Connell's superiors at the CIA knew about President Kennedy bringing Marilyn into meetings where Agency business was being discussed. However, we have to look at the way a CIA Officer would be placed into the position of talking over his plans in a room with Marilyn, because it does call into question her security clearance.

Once again I ask, why would John Kennedy bring Marilyn to these meetings? Did he know something about Marilyn nobody else knew? One thing is certain, the CIA and the FBI both developed a relationship with Marilyn Monroe and undoubtedly it was in their best interest to know what she was doing.

The CIA's charter bans domestic spying, but in 1976, the final report of the special Senate subcommittee, headed by Idaho Senator Frank Church, to investigate CIA abuses, concluded that the Agency had amassed files on more than 7,000 American citizens and 1,000 domestic organizations. That information was disseminated in thousands of reports to the FBI and other agencies.

Marilyn's house was bugged from February until the day she died. Any calls Robert Kennedy made to or from her house were being recorded. Spy games were running amok in Marilyn's world and looking back now, the final ending was predictable.

As early as 1963, the FBI and CIA knew of the Spindel and Otash electronic surveillance of Marilyn's house. The authorities must have heard from their sources that tapes were circulating, so they arrested Otash in an attempt to seize them. Their investigation into the John F. Kennedy assassination led them to believe that Otash had uncovered some link between Marilyn and the murder. It is a known fact that the FBI had its own recordings but found out that the Mafia and Jimmy Hoffa also had a copy.

Sam Giancana's assorted ties to John Kennedy have long been the theme of speculation. In 1960, Giancana was believed to have assisted in John F. Kennedy's Presidential election in Illinois. It appears the Chicago Mob boss had good reason to feel betrayed by the Kennedy Administration. The Attorney General was putting enormous legal pressure on Organized Crime.

However, the two had a nemesis in common, Fidel Castro. Mob leaders, who wanted to exploit Cuba's endless gambling potentials, hated Castro ever since he started governing that country. The US Government deemed his communist system of government, a hazard to national security, as evidenced by the Bay of Pigs invasion in April 1961. Marilyn's writings put US Government officials and Mob leaders in the same room, discussing how to get rid of this nemesis.

Giancana's personality had rubbed many people in the wrong way, possibly including Kennedy. Known as the man who orchestrated the infamous Valentine's Day Massacre, he was a ruthless assassin who rose to power by killing those who got in his way. He was assassinated himself in 1975, in the basement of his Illinois home in Oak Park; some suspected it was a hit by government agents.

Giancana was killed shortly before he was scheduled to appear before a U. S. Senate committee investigating an ostensible CIA and Mafia collusion in plots to assassinate President John F. Kennedy. Some commentators have alleged that the CIA killed Giancana because of his troubled history with the agency.

Another theory is that a New York crime family ordered Giancana's murder, due to fears that he would testify about Mafia. The other hit man, Johnny Roselli, who Marilyn wrote was involved in the CIA plots to kill Fidel Castro, was found stuffed in an oil drum floating off the coast of Miami. Remember the DA's investigator, Frank Hronek, who suspected the mafia? He uncovered evidence that Marilyn was murdered to keep her silent. This was the only public statement made by a government investigator, claiming there was another possible scenario to Marilyn's death. The evidence revealed is substantial, pointing to this conclusion, although there remain several conflicting stories as to what role the Mafia played that Saturday night in August.

The most condemning information we were able to obtain was from the wire-tapers and Sam Giancana's relatives, who wrote a book. How can your most incriminating evidence come from organized crime figures, and not from our own Law Enforcement agencies?

After Marilyn attended Frank Sinatra's party the weekend before her death, she wrote about drinking and talking too much. By all accounts, her conversations led Sam Giancana, the Al Capone of the 60's, to think he had major problems with Monroe's state of mind. During the party, she boasted about revealing the contents of her diary, which disclosed information regarding him working as an operative for the CIA.

This disclosure would cause serious concerns within his organization, and he hoped to hide it from other Mafia families. He had to make a move to protect his creditability. When Jimmy Hoffa told him he was going bug her house, he saw a perfect opportunity to silence Marilyn. The wire tapers said that they were afraid of the mobsters that Giancana sent, because they seemed more interested in killing Marilyn than anything else.

Bob said the most condemning part of the tapes was the interchange between Robert Kennedy and Marilyn as they were arguing about the whereabouts of the diary. After listening to the tapes, he asked did the wire tapers hear the murder being committed. They looked at each other and replied they didn't know, but he sensed certain uneasiness.

When the housekeeper found Marilyn unconscious, the wire tapers said they packed up and went home. If the death of Marilyn Monroe was recorded, the truth may only be revealed when and if one of these sets of tapes resurfaces. They could answer key questions about how Marilyn actually died, and provide clues about who killed her.

Researchers, writers, and law enforcement officials who claim to have heard some of these tapes or were told what was on them, have no doubt Marilyn was murdered. However they can only speculate as to who actually did it.

Most of the theories involve the mobsters from the wiretaps, Robert Kennedy, Secret Service, or Johnny Roselli with J. Edgar Hoover watching and listening.

Surprisingly not one of these audiotapes has ever been made public. Obviously CIA and FBI wiretaps were classified as matters of national security, but the mafia tapes were different. What happened to those recordings? We can assume that Hoffa got a copy of all the tapes because he paid for the endeavor. Spindel and Otash each got their own because they were able to duplicate them. I believe the very intimidating Giancana got one as well. However, many other copies were made from these masters and we know they were edited due to the amount of hours recorded. Where are they now?

It is obvious that Hoffa used his tape to try to blackmail someone in the Justice Department, because Robert Kennedy decided to halt his investigation into the government's charges against Hoffa. After his brother was murdered, he didn't have the same interest or power. It was not until he resigned as Attorney General and started his bid for a seat in the United States Senate that the Hoffa conviction was realized.

Many people who were involved in this investigation have died. John and Robert Kennedy were murdered in front of numerous witnesses, Sam Giancana was murdered in his kitchen, Bernard Spindel died mysteriously while in jail, and Jimmy Hoffa simply disappeared and rumored to have been buried under a stadium. At least Marilyn died in her bedroom, but are we to assume these events were all a coincidence?

> Marilyn was murdered in 1962.
>
> John Kennedy was murdered in 1963.
>
> Robert Kennedy was murdered in 1968.
>
> Bernard Spindel died in 1968.
>
> Jimmy Hoffa disappeared in 1974.
>
> Sam Giancana was killed in 1975.

Spindel died while serving time for illegally tapping the phone of a prominent New York attorney. The cause of death was reported to be a heart attack at the age of forty-five. According to his wife, it was a consequence of prison officials failing to give him his medicine.

New York County (Manhattan) District Attorney Frank S. Hogan confiscated Spindel's tapes and files at his home. Now get this, Bernard bugged his own house. When the detectives served the subpoena, he activated the recorder and taped them saying, "Find the Marilyn files."

Mrs. Spindel once claimed she had positive proof from taped conversations amongst the police, who talked about the Marilyn Monroe connection while at her house. Her husband's files on Monroe and Bobby Kennedy were amongst the things they were looking for.

The December 21, 1966, New York Times ran a three-column story by Robert Tomasson.

Tomasson wrote:

"In a affidavit submitted to the court, Bernard Spindel had filed suit for the return of bugging devices and tapes of Marilyn Monroe. He asserted that some of material contained tapes and evidence containing the circumstances surrounding the cause of death of Marilyn Monroe."

The New York District of Attorney's Office responded by saying the evidence was lost. But they didn't know Spindel. He not only had copies stashed all over New York, but had tapes of the raid on his house that showed the FBI was involved.

In 1992, the Los Angeles Times ran a story written by Myrna Oliver, A Times Staff Writer. She wrote in part;

Fred Otash; Colorful Hollywood Private Eye and Author

"Fred Otash, legendary Hollywood vice cop and private eye has died at the age of 70. The colorful Otash, who had just completed a book titled "Marilyn, Kennedy, and Me" about the death of Marilyn Monroe, died Monday in his West Hollywood home of natural causes. Otash is rumored to have been one of the investigators who kept a physical and electronic surveillance on Marilyn Monroe in the months before her death."

In 1976 his book, Investigation Hollywood: Memoirs Of

Hollywood's Top Private Detective, was published. Otash claimed in this book that after President Kennedy was assassinated, the FBI confiscated files he maintained on Kennedy. In 1963, he was arrested for not revealing information on who else was involved in the conspiracy to kill Marilyn and Kennedy.

I often wondered why Albert Stiller made a point of saying the Secret Service wanted to talk to me. Although they never approached me, just the mention of them was cause for concern. Deputy Lester Goldberg had talked to them, Milo had pointed a finger at them in his book, and Bob had accused them of the murder.

One would figure that the two agents who came to the Coroner's Office were Kennedy's men, looking for the journal that Marilyn was supposed to have. The agency was said to be a wing of White House security, but probably owed some of their allegiance to the U.S. Army that trained them. United States Army Intelligence had a big stake in this game because of the nuclear weapons issue in Cuba.

A short time after Marilyn died, John Kennedy would face one of the biggest challenges of his life. He woke up one morning and found tactical nuclear weapons ninety miles off the coast of the United States. The Soviet field commanders who operated the missiles were authorized to use them if Cuba was invaded by the United States. The fate of millions literally hinged upon the ability of the President to navigate the right course of action.

All of available research suggests that the U.S. first obtained photographic evidence of the missiles in October, when a CIA U-2 pilot captured images of what were identified as medium range ballistic missiles. When the President was briefed on the CIA's analysis of the images, Kennedy chose to use a U.S. Naval quarantine of foreign ships carrying offensive weapons for Cuba, as opposed to a blockade of all materials heading for their ports. A classic blockade could not be used, because it would of had to take place in international waters.

The Soviets responded to the quarantine by sending 14 ships presumably carrying weapons to Cuba. Kennedy issued a stern statement that he would send his nuclear armed Navy to intercept the Soviet armada. The world held its breath as the two most powerful countries headed for their meeting in the Atlantic Ocean. Thank God the Soviets blinked and turned back to Russia, averting a possible calamity.

It was rumored that even on the brink of his meeting with destiny, Kennedy was occupied with his newest love.

When the CIA came to notify the President of the crisis, the Secret Service informed them that there was a 'Do Not Disturb' sign on his private room in the White House and advising them to take the report of nuclear weapons in Cuba to Secretary of State, Robert McNamara.

You can imagine what the Generals of the United States Army and the Admirals of the United States Navy thought about the leader the voters had sent them. The relationship had started off bad with the Bay of Pigs, and although the planning wasn't his, it was still Kennedy's responsibility, as Commander-in-Chief, to finalize the operation. When the CIA was thrown out of Cuba, the Army wanted to invade and get their prestige back. They never forgave President Kennedy for opposing them.

The strong military complex that former President Dwight Eisenhower had warned Americans about was beginning to flex its muscles. Maybe the military wanted to take an active role in running the government. I remember when one of America's most gifted Generals, Alexander Haig, was chosen as Secretary of State. President Reagan was shot and when the Vice President was unavailable, he brazenly stated,

"I've got everything under control," and America shuttered.

To the American public, Kennedy was a hero. His Administration had averted a nuclear war when the military complex wanted a confrontation. He was killed a few months later, after only a little more than 2 years in office. Not since Abraham Lincoln's assassination had America mourned so deeply for the death of a President. The political rock star was gone. Gone was Camelot. But his hope for America still lived.

CHAPTER 15:
The Usual Suspects

Life has a way of funny sweeping you in directions you could never imagine. Who would have thought Robert Slatzer and I would have crossed paths like we did in 1974, nearly twelve years after my Coroner's Office experience. Up until then, only the assassinations of John and Robert Kennedy had offered any clues to her death. By then, I honestly believed the case of Marilyn Monroe was completely dead. My mind was made up to stay out of that mass of confusion.

However, Bob's passion for bringing justice to Marilyn inspired me. His sincerity and dedication to this task was infectious. Nobody cared about Marilyn Monroe more than Robert Slatzer. He told me that he and Marilyn met at Fox Studio's lot when she was a model. On a weekend rendezvous in Ensenada Mexico, they married and returned to California. When Twentieth Century Fox discovered it, they undid the marriage by burning the copy of the certificate filed in Mexican courts.

A native of Marion, Ohio, Bob attended Ohio State University and began his writing career as a reporter for the Scripps Howard newspapers. He came to Hollywood in

1946 to write about the movie business, and eventually found work in films as a screenwriter, director, and producer. He wrote and directed a number of "B" movies. In addition, he wrote a book called "Duke: The Life and Times of John Wayne" and another called "Bing Crosby: Hollow Man."

In 1974, Bob had written and his publisher was releasing, "The Life and Curious Death of Marilyn Monroe". On the promotional tour for this very revealing story, he walked into a studio where I was producing a Public Affairs program. We struck up a friendship that lasted until his death in 2005. I remember talking to Bob after his surgery and him telling me to write a book or sell the idea of a feature film to a producer in order to document what we had been doing for the last thirty years.

Bob said he would try to live long enough to help me, but of course this wasn't to be the case. He told me to keep on telling what happened in the Coroner's Office and disclose what I know about the diary, because he knew I had not told it all. Marilyn's writings were the one thing we had in common over the years, because we had both seen it. I always had the feeling Bob was uncomfortable with her dealings with the CIA and the FBI. When the question of Castro or Sukarno came up, he never had anything to say about them.

In response to my question did he think Marilyn was a communist, he answered no way. We never discussed any of the FBI entries regarding the House Un American

Committee, but there was no doubt that Bob had benefited from the Congressional attack on European and Jewish writers. Bob had come to Hollywood as a red white, and blue American from the Midwest, and got some of the writing jobs left open because publishers and studios would not hire an accused communist.

His problems began when, according to him, he married Marilyn and came up against one of Fox Studios potential moneymakers. He was never interested in the other side of her existence, but only who killed her and removing the negativity associated with the suicide aspect of her death. So the true realities of her life were not discussed, and left to other journalists to investigate. I'm not a journalist, but have researched what was in the diary and have developed some interesting conclusions.

The information I have gathered since 1962 convinced me that the secrets of Marilyn's life and death were spelled out in that diary. At first, I viewed Marilyn's notes as newsworthy, but intimidating. As the years went by, its importance became increasingly obvious. I began to understand that Marilyn was writing about policy that impacted the fabric of America.

From Marilyn's time with Arthur Miller, while working for the FBI to her escapades with the Kennedy brothers, she was in the middle of serious political activities with far reaching consequences. The diary detailed these periods of her life in a uniquely profound way. Marilyn's writings were more than just a personal journal; they provided a spellbinding glimpse into the high stakes world in which we all live.

Even as stories of sex parties began to appear, it never swayed my opinion of the social value of her writings. I never felt any inclination to connect America's enduring movie star and sex symbol to the murky world of international skullduggery. After all, her legacy has endured 50 years of controversy since her death, and she is still America's sweetheart. However, with that said, the significance of the information in her diary cannot be overlooked.

Kennedy, the Secret Service Agents, and Peter Lawford had searched Marilyn's house looking for her diary. The CIA and FBI both had wiretaps presumably looking for the same thing. Jimmy Hoffa and Sam Giancana sent wire tappers and Mafia hit men to find it. Without a doubt, if that diary had not disappeared from the Coroner's Office and been made public, its impact would have altered future events in ways unimaginable.

Over the years, the growing relevance of her journal has continued to amaze me. Maybe if I would have had time to read the whole book, there might have been more revelations in it. The general consensus was that someone with a key or combination to the safe at the Coroner's Office took it out of circulation, but you never can tell.

The architects of the Marilyn Monroe cover-up were active participants in her death right from the start. A good indication of this was the story that was concocted about that night and how shallow the official police investigation has been ever since.

It is hard to figure out what the Los Angeles Police Department knew, because they never made the results public. Although they had some of their top detectives investigating her case, the only witnesses ever spoken to were Marilyn's doctors and housekeeper. Jack Clemmons once told me that the Los Angeles Police Department's investigation of Marilyn's death was shameful and you could smell the stench of a cover-up all the way to the White House.

In 1993, Bob Slatzer and I went to Police Headquarters for an updated file regarding her case and were told no official report on Marilyn's death existed. Why wouldn't there be a public file on Marilyn's death?

Constitutional law researchers have made the individual's rights a point of contention against the United States Government's interest in protecting an intelligence asset. In 2010, a new document was released under the Freedom of Information Act, verifying the CIA was bugging Marilyn's house the night she died. But how does the Freedom of Information Act relate to local government in particular with Marilyn Monroe's death?

Marilyn's writings and my subsequent investigation have shown many complications, which could have influenced Los Angeles Police Department, County Coroner, and District

Attorney Investigations. Although some of the specifics remain unclear, the cast of characters who participated in the cover up and, or death of Marilyn Monroe has become unmistakable.

Here's the list of usual suspects:

The Kennedy Family

Marilyn's relationship with the Kennedy's is the most plausible reason for her death. From her introduction to John in the late 50's until the night she died, Marilyn became entrenched in a world for which there was no escape. Not for her, and ultimately not for John or Robert Kennedy either. These three were destined to die within 6 years of each other, and each under shadowy circumstances.

Although her relationship with Bobby Kennedy seems more directly related to her death, it was his brother John who really placed her in harms way when he brought her to CIA meetings with the Mafia. Why bring her to those meetings? Did Marilyn have a security clearance? Was she already a briefed and active member of the U.S. Intelligence community? Whatever the answers, Marilyn would end up representing a security threat that sent the Federal Bureau of Investigations and Central Intelligence Agency scurrying to wiretap her house and telephones.

By all accounts, Marilyn was genuinely in love with Bobby Kennedy and believed he was going leave his wife to marry her. Her last days with Bobby were a sad commentary to their overall relationship. Marilyn's best friend, Jeanne Carmine, once told me that Marilyn's affair with John Kennedy was all fun and games. They partied around town; everyone in the Industry knew about their relationship. However, with Bobby it was much different. Carmine said Marilyn fell hard for him and she remembers them "kissing madly" during special moments they shared.

Another of Marilyn's good friends, Terry Moore, said Marilyn really believed Bobby loved her and that one day he would become President of the United States, and she his First Lady. Their relationship was secretive, but her friends were present many times when they were together.

Jeanne described being there when Bobby first discovered Marilyn was keeping a journal of her activities with him. She said Bobby had come over to Marilyn's place and found the diary lying on the table. She recalled him being livid and confronting Marilyn about the book. "What is this," he asked her. Marilyn related that it was her diary and she wanted to be able to remember things so she could talk to him later about it. Carmine said Kennedy told her, "Get rid of it. Get rid of it now!"

The night of Marilyn's death, Bobby Kennedy and Peter Lawford were at Marilyn's house according to multiple eyewitness accounts. According to her diary and wiretap recordings, a violent argument occurred between Marilyn and Bobby. What happened after the argument and fight is sketchy, but wiretap evidence suggests that secret service agents may have sedated Marilyn before leaving the premises.

After her mysterious death, the Kennedy family began to handle the cover-up of Bobby being at the house the night she died. They also sought to play down any reference to John Kennedy's relationship with Marilyn from 1958 through 1962. It was a masterful job by professionals with unlimited resources and the ability to reach almost anybody. They stonewalled every investigation by local law enforcement officials, and even after JFK's assassination, the cover up continued on.

With all that was known, the Kennedy connection was the logical place for investigators to start. But with White House denials, there were no facts to be found for their investigations. The Kennedy name made for great gossip and excited the public's imagination, but the reality was that no one could get any answers from them.

Let's develop one conspiracy theory from my experiences and research. I've mentioned that there are some links between the Kennedys' assassinations and Marilyn's death. There weren't enough ears to hear all the rumors, both real and imagined, but here's one that I've developed.

November 1960: Senator John F. Kennedy defeats Vice President Nixon in a close presidential election. Kennedy went ahead with the secret Nixon-Hunt plans for a CIA-backed invasion of Cuba. Howard Hunt was reportedly at Kennedy's side during the execution phase of the endeavor.

The invasion at the Bay of Pigs would be a monumental

failure. CIA and Cuban exile leaders, such as Eugenio, blamed Kennedy for withholding planned military air cover. Kennedy threatens to dismantle the agency, but opts to hire a new director instead. However, the friction from this incident would continue to simmer.

Meanwhile, Marilyn was also engaged in secret operations with the CIA. She makes a trip to Mexico City and attends a Fair Play For Cuba committee meeting. While there she meets Lee Harvey Oswald, who is also working for the agency. She learns information that sends U.S. Intelligence operations into a mass frenzy.

Upon returning home, her entire house is bugged and conversations are recorded between her and Bobby Kennedy, discussing obviously sensitive information. Marilyn is also heard talking to members of the American Communist Party in Mexico City.

Joseph Kennedy, the patriarch of the family becomes aware of the threat Marilyn represents to his sons, and the entire Kennedy family. Joe, who had made his fortune during the prohibition era, had genuine ties to organized crime. He gained some sort of legitimacy when he was appointed ambassador to Great Britain, but even then he was suspected of Nazi ties by the British.

There is evidence suggesting that Joe had taken out a contract, with Sam Giancana to murder Marilyn. After Giancana had fulfilled his contract, he expected the Kennedy Administration to ease off their prosecution efforts against him, Jimmy Hoffa, and other organized crime members. This never happened.

The CIA and the Mafia would then conspire to kill President Kennedy, and use Lee Harvey Oswald as their fall guy. Oswald would then be brazenly murdered by one of Giancana's hit men. We know that this would not have been the first time CIA operatives and mafia members worked together.

At the time, Robert Kennedy was powerless to do anything about his brother's murder. However a few years later he was on the verge of becoming President of the United States, which would have given him the power to expose the truth. This would have had far reaching ramifications, shaking the very foundation of our Nation. U.S. Intelligence could not allow that to happen, so Robert Kennedy was assassinated as well.

If ordered, Howard Hunt, Robert Maheu, and Jim O'Connell, would not have hesitated to kill anybody, and Giancana or Roselli would have done the same if paid. Marilyn and the Kennedy's lives were each intertwined and all paid the price.

In the mid 90's, a collection of documents supposedly written by John Kennedy to Marilyn Monroe surfaced. These were known as the Cusack Papers, purportedly written by Kennedy in his own hand, discussing the relationship between him, Marilyn Monroe and the Chicago gangster Sam Giancana.

According to Lawrence Cusack, he found these documents in the attic of his deceased father's house. He states that his father died in 1985 after having served as a secret counselor to Kennedy. He claims that these correspondences were love letters and secret communications between the President and Marilyn Monroe.

The documents were later deemed to be forged after more than 350 of them were sold. In 1999, Cusack was found guilty of fraud and sentenced to ten years in prison. Many feel that Mr. Cusack was punished wrongfully, and I am certainly one of those who understand that sentiment.

In 1962, Deputy Danbacker told me Marilyn's file cabinet had been broken into. In 1974, Bob Slatzer had told me about going to Marilyn's house days after her death and discovering the same. He also claimed Marilyn told him about some love letters she was keeping. It's possible these Cusack Papers were part of what was taken out of Marilyn's cabinet, and the Kennedy machine had managed to maintain the cover up once again.

After his conviction, the Kennedy family sought to have these documents destroyed. They stated that there was a significant risk that the forgeries will re-enter the market place and the only way to prevent this was to destroy them.

Others feel that even though they may be forgeries, they in themselves were a piece of history. Many have spent considerable sums of money and want the documents returned, stating that these documents have not been tested appropriately. I never heard the outcome of this case, but it proves the cover-up continues into 21ˢᵗ century.

Peter Lawford

Peter Lawford was a British-born actor, who most people born after 1970 would never remember. Achieving acting fame as a child, Lawford appeared in numerous movies during the 1940's and 50's, eventually becoming part of the famous "Rat Pack" including Frank Sinatra, Dean Martin, Sammy Davis Jr., and Joey Bishop. However, Lawford's biggest role didn't happen on the big screen, but occurred in real life during his involvement with Marilyn Monroe and the Kennedys.

In 1954, Peter Lawford married Patricia Kennedy, sister of then U.S. Senator John Kennedy. At that time Lawford was not a US citizen, but had married into one of the country's most influential families. Lawford, along with Frank Sinatra, played huge roles in fundraising for JFK's presidential campaign. Eventually Lawford would become the ultimate front man for the entire Kennedy family. He became the protector of their family image, and the Kennedy brothers' link to Hollywood glamour.

Lawford befriended Marilyn and she spent considerable time at his home. In fact, she spent so much time there that J Edgar Hoover wiretapped Lawford's house, according to FBI disclosures. Entries in Marilyn's diary and wiretaps reveal he was fully aware of Marilyn's intentions to hold a press conference and pleaded with her to call it off.

There are conflicting stories about Lawford's whereabouts the evening Marilyn died, but according to her last diary entries and wiretap recordings, Lawford was at Marilyn's house that night. According to White House telephone logs, he called President Kennedy at 6:04AM the morning of her death. No doubt he was keeping the President abreast of the situation with Marilyn.

If anyone subscribes to the theory that Robert Kennedy had a role in Marilyn's death, then Peter Lawford would have been his chief conspirator. Many believe that Lawford handled the clean up at the crime scene while convincing both doctors and the housekeeper to lie to investigators in the interest of national security.

Amazingly, just a few years later, Peter Lawford's name was associated with another well-known celebrity, who died under more than mysterious circumstances. Dorothy Dandridge had been dating Lawford before her death. She was found dead at her home from an apparent self-administered drug overdose. A proclaimed suicide note was found, but its authenticity was later questioned. However, no serious investigation was ever performed, and Dr. Theodore Curphey ruled her death an overdose from the anti-depressant drug Tofranil.

A subsequent examination would later show conflicting evidence as to how she died. As for Peter Lawford, who was still married to Patricia Kennedy at the time, his wife would file for a divorce less than a year after Dorothy Dandridge's death. Whether her death was accidental, suicidal, or something else remains a mystery to this very day.

Sam Giancana

Sam Giancana was a Sicilian American mobster and boss of the notorious "Chicago Outfit." During the 1950's, Giancana along with other crime bosses began setting their sights on building gambling casinos in Havana, Cuba. These mobsters, hoping to make millions, were negotiating with the Cuban President Fulgencio Batista, a U.S. friendly dictator.

Before their enterprising plans could be completed, a revolution began taking place in Cuba. This uprising, being fought by the country's peasants and farmers, was led by a man named Fidel Castro. Castro, being lauded as a champion of anti-imperialism, spearheaded the charge to ouster the system of inequality gripping their Caribbean Island.

The Central Intelligence Agency and the U.S. Government were also feeling the pinch of Castro's revolution. Many U.S. and European countries were heavily vested in Batista's presidency and wanted something done to prevent his overthrow. Big Jim O'Connell was appointed by CIA officials to head up a plot to kill Fidel Castro. O'Connell then turned to the intelligence communities' number one operative, Robert Maheu.

Maheu, who was based in Las Vegas, then began orchestrating a plan that would ultimately lead to Sam Giancana's involvement with Marilyn Monroe. Being the smooth operative he was, Maheu put together an unprecedented plan to hire mobsters, who would assassinate Fidel Castro. CIA documents have revealed Maheu was close associates with mobster hit man Johnny Roselli, who knew him as a Las Vegas bigwig rolling with billionaire tycoon, Howard Hughes.

Maheu told Roselli about international businessman willing to pay $150,000 for a Castro hit. Roselli then set up a meeting attended by Giancana, Roselli, Maheu, and Big Jim O'Connell. By most accounts, these mobsters would make subsequent attempts to assassinate the Cuban leader, but were obviously never successful.

When John Kennedy was elected to President, Cuba was the nation's hottest crisis and O'Connell needed to brief him on what the CIA had in mind for Castro. Kennedy anticipated a showdown with the Cuban leader and told O'Connell to set up additional meetings with Giancana and Roselli.

Marilyn Monroe attended at least two of these meetings. Not only does she describe them in her diary, but CIA disclosures have confirmed these meetings took place as well. Sam Giancana was never happy about Kennedy bringing Marilyn to these meetings. This was a tenuous situation for him, working in cahoots with the U.S. Government. If the other crime families were to find out, they would not have been pleased. Marilyn was an unexpected wildcard that Giancana never saw coming.

Flash forward two years and Giancana's worst fear was becoming a reality. Marilyn carelessly liked to dress up and go to Frank Sinatra's lavish parties; she shows up at one of these parties the weekend before she dies. While there, Marilyn gets drunk as hell and starts talking about holding a press conference to reveal everything about the Kennedys. Giancana became livid and decided he needed to quickly do something about this pestilent situation.

Union Boss Jimmy Hoffa also attended that Frank Sinatra party. He knew of Marilyn's connection with the Kennedys and apparently wanted to use her for getting a foothold in the Justice Department. Together they would develop a plan to murder her and blame it on Bobby Kennedy.

The first part of the plan was to have Teamster President Jimmy Hoffa hire Bernard Spindel and Fred Otash to bug Marilyn's house. Hoffa's initial target was her diary, needing it for leverage. However, these wire tappers were unaware that the total plan was to murder her.

The second part was to listen for the opportune moment, and then unleash Giancana's professional hit men on Marilyn. If the plan had worked, Monroe would be dead and Robert Kennedy blamed. Jimmy Hoffa would then have a shot at blackmailing the government into dropping the charges against him, and Sam Giancana would have shut Marilyn up for good.

As U.S. Attorney General, Robert was actively trying to convict Hoffa for his shady union practices. He didn't know he had also become the target of a sinister plot to get rid of Marilyn and completely disgrace his own family.

Now the question remains, did Giancana contact Robert Maheu or Jim O'Connell too complain about Marilyn's threats? We know they were all plotting together to kill Castro with a suppository. We also know that the CIA and FBI had wiretap lines at Marilyn's home. Was Marilyn a big enough threat to warrant a decision to kill her by intelligence and mafia members? Certainly the Central Intelligence Agency had the power to orchestrate a cover up of this magnitude, and Sam Giancana had the resources to make sure nobody ever heard anything from Marilyn again.

As a footnote to this story, when Lee Harvey Oswald allegedly assassinated President Kennedy, a man employed by Sam Giancana named Jack Ruby, gunned down Oswald before he could ever be taken to trial.

A few years later, one of Giancana's relatives was quoted in the Los Angeles Times, saying he killed Marilyn with a suppository in the rectum. He later died in his jail cell. Why am I not surprised?

Robert Maheu

Robert Maheu may be the Keyser Söze of this whodunit. In fact, the only constant throughout this investigation has been Maheu, and the more we examine his role, the more he appears to be the puppet master of this twisted tale. Remember, all of this began with Maheu, who also known as, "Iron Bob". He introduced his self to Marilyn as a Federal Bureau of Investigations agent who, as she put it, "wanted me to do something for America." Maheu would then ask Marilyn to gather information about the communist activities of Arthur Miller, promising her a lucrative film deal in return.

He first approached her in the early to mid fifties, when she knew nothing about the Kennedys, or the intelligence community. Marilyn was just another young, struggling Hollywood actress full of insecurities, seeking stardom and willing to do almost anything to achieve it.

Maheu already had his operation in place when he introduced himself to Marilyn. Paula Strasberg was part of the team, employed to cozy up to Marilyn. Maheu made sure their relationship got even cozier. It was Strasberg who convinced Marilyn that working with him was the right thing to do. She taught Marilyn about the inner workings of communism, including the language, organization, and what information Maheu and the Federal Bureau of Investigations were looking for.

After Marilyn successfully allowed the government to

bring charges against Arthur Miller, she was introduced to John F. Kennedy. You have to question the occurrence and timing of this introduction. Kennedy was well known from his Harvard days as a playboy. It was like sending a lamb to slaughter. The only question is, who really got slaughtered?

All available evidence suggests that Robert Maheu arranged to have Marilyn introduced to John Kennedy. Although called a close friend and confidant of the Kennedys, the facts point to something different. Maheu was a double agent, who worked for both the FBI and CIA. Prior to the Kennedy presidency, he was already involved with the revolution taking place in Cuba. The Central Intelligence Agency was concerned about whether the new administration would continue to support their clandestine efforts in that country.

Maheu's spy work brought him in contact with Howard Hughes. Hughes was the CIA's largest contractor and proclaimed richest man in the world. He was a renowned playboy and filmmaker who discovered movie goddesses Jane Russell and Jean Harlow. Hughes was once married to one of Marilyn's close friends, actress Terry Moore, in the early 1950's.

In my research, Maheu appeared to be the contact that government agencies relied on for the dirty jobs. FBI disclosures have now revealed that no other than J. Edgar Hoover implicated Maheu being involved with Robert Kennedy's assassination.

In testimony before the U.S. Senate Select Committee on Intelligence in 1975, Maheu defended his role in any assassination scheme as an act of patriotism. The ex-CIA operative used his connection to the hits and his relationship with the Agency to evade legal difficulties. He was charged with wiretapping Sam Giancana's girlfriend's room. The charges stemmed from Maheu hiring men to bug the room of Phyllis McGuire of the singing McGuire sisters. He told the FBI that he was bugging her to see if she was leaking details about the CIA/Mafia hits on Castro.

Many facts remain unclear about Robert Maheu, but some things are certain. Maheu was a paid operative and assassin working for the intelligence wing of United States Government. He obviously was implementing a specific agenda right from the start, and nothing or nobody was going to get in his way. The fact that the nation's top lawman, J. Edgar Hoover, who Maheu had worked for, believed he orchestrated the Robert Kennedy assassination is quite telling within itself. The distinct possibility exist that Robert Maheu was directly involved in the deaths of Marilyn Monroe and both of the Kennedys. Killing is what he did best and in his twisted view of national security, tying off the loose ends these three represented would have been easy to justify.

Paula Strasberg

In 1955, with the help of Robert Maheu and the FBI, Monroe negotiated a new contract with 20th Century Fox to make four films over a seven-year period. The first film to be made under the contract was "Bus Stop", directed by Joshua Logan. In Logan's autobiography *Movie Stars, Real People and Me,* director Logan wrote:

> *"I found Marilyn to be one of the great talents of all time. She struck me as being a much brighter person than I had ever imagined, and I think that was the first time I learned that intelligence and, yes, brilliance have nothing to do with education."*

During that time, Monroe severed contact with her drama coach, Natasha Lytess, replacing her with Paula Strasberg. During the filming of Monroe's subsequent films, Strasberg would become a constant presence.

Laurence Olivier directed and starred in Marilyn's next film, "The Prince and the Showgirl". However, during filming Olivier resented Monroe's dependence on Paula Strasberg, regarding the coach as a fraud whose only talent was the ability to "butter Marilyn up". He recalled his attempts at explaining a scene to Monroe, only to hear Strasberg interject, "Honey - just think of Coca-Cola and Frank Sinatra."

On one occasion, Arthur Miller remembered Strasberg telling Marilyn: "You are the greatest woman of your time, the greatest human being of your time; of any time, you name it." With this kind of encouragement from Strasberg, it was easy to see why Marilyn embraced her image.

Paula had recently been blacklisted as a communist by the House Un American Activities Committee, but worked hard to become the only person Marilyn trusted. With Robert Maheu at the controls, Paula also began teaching Marilyn the inner workings of the Communist movement.

Marilyn would learn exactly what information the FBI was looking for and how to get it.

When the relationship between Monroe and Miller was developing, the press began to write about them as a couple. As rumors of their impending marriage began to surface, they became the targets of excessive media interest. They were eventually married on June 29, 1956.

The reports of marriage and romance were soon overtaken by news that Miller had been called to testify before the House Un-American Activities Committee. He was subpoenaed to explain his supposed communist affiliations with members of Group Theatre. Miller was ordered to testify before the Committee, because Maheu and Strasberg convinced Marilyn to get information about Miller's friends and activities. Miller refused the demand to identify communists he was acquainted with and was consequently charged with contempt of Congress. Paula's husband, Lee Strasberg, was a former member of Group

Theatre. When they came under fire from the committee, he formed Actors Studio, which was quickly joined by many of the top actors of that time. Although he proclaimed it was not really an extension of Group Theatre, the leftist political orientation could not be denied.

According to Marilyn's diary, Miller was urged by the Strasbergs to cooperate with the committee through the FBI. However, Miller refused and branded the couple as "snitches." Marilyn's writings also expressed regret for "letting them use her" to set up Miller. During the hearings, she paid many of his legal bills, and remained by his side through out the process. After Arthur Miller won his appeal and filmed "The Misfits" with Marilyn, they ended their relationship with the Strasbergs and each other.

Dr. Theodore Curphey

My first direct encounter with Dr. Theodore Curphey came only 2 weeks after being employed by the Los Angeles County Coroner's Office. George Reeves, the actor who played the original "Superman", had been found dead. Family members were saying he was murdered, and Dr. Curphey was calling it suicide. Somehow I ended up in the middle.

Welcome to the Los Angeles County Coroner's Office. Only weeks after I arrived, this case had thrust me into controversy. I did not have the experience or the authority to question the police about the evidence at the scene or the observations of those who knew something about the circumstances.

My first interaction with Dr. Curphey went smoothly, unlike many of the others in the office. Looking back, if I would have questioned him about the Reeves evidence, Curphey and I may have clashed on this one as well. During the next two years, we disagreed on at least twenty cases including Ronald Stokes, Ernie Kovacs, and many other controversial deaths. I guess my attention to detail didn't allow for County regulations to be ignored. When they handed me that deputy badge and the book containing its legal responsibilities, it was my goal to follow the letter of the law. This didn't sit well with the politics of the office because regulations were viewed like guidelines rather than law.

Enter the death of Marilyn Monroe. Conspirators involved in this case never intended for the Coroner's office to receive Marilyn's body. In fact, every effort had been made to prevent this from happening. Once her body arrived, a cascading chain of events began to take place. This unfortunately placed Dr. Curphey in a compromising situation.

On Tuesday August 7, the day Dr. Thomas Noguchi performed the autopsy on Marilyn, Dr. Curphey announced that a massive overdose of barbiturates was the cause of death. He claimed she had ingested lethal doses of both Nembutal and Chloral Hydrate, and either could have killed her. The problem with his statement was that the preliminary toxicology report had found no poison in Marilyn's stomach and secondary toxicology reports were not complete. No mention of Chloral Hydrate had previously been revealed, so how did Dr. Curphey come to these early conclusions?

Curphey then assigned her case to the Suicide Investigation Team, led by a group of doctors from the Suicide Prevention Center. This was an organziation co-founded by Dr. Curphey. During my investigation, he told me to provide them with anything they needed, which basically turned out to be setting up a press conference one week later to announce their findings. On August 17, 1962, a packed room of newsmen from around the world were told Marilyn's death was a probable suicide.

After that press conference, Dr. Curphey moved straight ahead with closing Marilyn's case. He ordered me to gather what documents were available, disregard those that weren't, and sign the death certificate. The actions of Dr. Theodore Curphey, while handling the Marilyn Monroe case, constituted a breach of the County Coroner's investigative responsibility and a cover-up of the facts surrounding her death. This was the part of Marilyn's case witnessed first-hand by me.

After his retirement from the Los Angeles County Coroner's Office in 1967, Dr. Curphey served as a forensic medicine consultant and with the Suicide Prevention Center.

As far as I know, he never publicly commented on the truth or anything else about Marilyn's death.

Dr. Ralph Greenson and Dr. Myron Engelberg

One of the most intriguing characters in this story is Marilyn's Psychiatrist Dr. Ralph Greenson. When examining his role in her death, many questions are left unanswered with the lingering feeling that he was much more involved than meets the eye.

Ralph Greenson, born Romeo Greenschpoon, was a prominent psychoanalyst who studied medicine in Switzerland. He was listed as a member of the Communist International Party, and was very popular with many Hollywood celebrities. Greenson was introduced to Marilyn Monroe in 1960, not long after she began hanging out with John Kennedy. According to her diary and Bob Slatzer, this introduction came by way of Frank Sinatra during the filming of Arthur Miller's "The Misfits".

She wrote in her diary,

"I wonder if Frank knew he was a party member."

Frank Sinatra's name has continued to pop up during my investigation. Sinatra garnered considerable attention due to his alleged personal and professional links with organized crime, including figures such as Sam Giancana. The Federal Bureau of Investigation kept records amounting to 2,403 pages on Sinatra. In relation to Marilyn's case, his alleged Mafia ties may only be equaled by his friendship with John F. Kennedy. During his election campaign, Sinatra was one of Kennedy's biggest fundraisers.

After Sinatra introduced Marilyn to Dr. Greenson, she became his patient. This made Greenson one of the most important Communist operatives in America. He had access to the mind of a woman involved in matters of national security. Greenson was well positioned to gather intelligence from every aspect of Marilyn's life, and he help place other key people around her to make his surveillance complete.

Greenson recommended Dr. Hyman Engelberg as her primary physician and strongly suggested Marilyn hiring Eunice Murray as her housekeeper. Coincidently, both were members of the Communist Party and her housekeeper's brother, Churchill Murray, was another person under surveillance by the FBI and the CIA. He introduced Monroe to Cuban diplomats in Mexico City.

Dr. Ralph Greenson, like many of his colleagues at the time, relied heavily on drug therapy for his patients. He routinely ordered prescriptions for barbiturates and tranquilizers. He referred Marilyn to Dr. Engelberg, who prescribed most of the medications Greenson ordered for her.

Marilyn's friends noticed that the more she saw Greenson, the more miserable she became. Jeanne Carmine and Terry Moore both described how she deteriorated under

Greenson's care, becoming insecure and depressed.

On the night of Marilyn's death, Dr. Greenson was strangely the first doctor called and not her primary physician Dr. Engelberg. According to Greenson, upon his arrival, he broke her bedroom window, climbed through, and did nothing else except remove the phone from her hand. When Jack Clemmons arrived on the scene, Greenson pointed to the empty prescription containers on the table next to her and simply said, "She must have taken all these."

Engelberg, who was described by police as despondent after examining Monroe's body, discussed her battle with manic depression and chemical dependency with the Los Angeles County Coroner and Suicide Investigation Team. Both doctors reportedly told investigators she was suicidal and died as a result of a drug overdose.

At later times, both doctors would recant ever saying Marilyn was suicidal or that they believed her death was suicide. But questions remain as to why they took so long to call the police after discovering her body and why they lied to Police and Coroner's investigators. Perhaps the biggest mystery of all was who prescribed the chloral hydrate that killed Marilyn.

Engelberg told the Los Angeles Times that he had prescribed Nembutal capsules only two or three days before her death, and that she was to take one each night to help her sleep. A 50-capsule bottle of the sedative, among some seven or eight other medicine bottles, were all found empty on her nightstand. He also stated that he was surprised to see that many empty containers and that his Nembutal prescription was for only 25 pills. Engelberg claimed he never prescribed any choral hydrate.

Los Angeles County Coroner Theodore J. Curphey said after an autopsy that his "presumptive opinion" was that death was due to an overdose of some drug. He opted not to conduct a formal inquest, but instead appointed a three-member team of mental health professionals to probe into her background. They also concluded her death was a probable suicide. These conclusions were based largely upon the testimony of Marilyn's doctors.

Whatever Greenson's role in the cover up of her death, his overall involvement had profound implications. Obviously Monroe knew a great deal about the behind-the-scenes world of American politics, but the question remains how much she had told her psychoanalyst.

Being a devout communist, Ralph Greenson wanted all the latest gossip from Marilyn regarding her secret conversations with Robert and John Kennedy. He also had Marilyn record many audiocassettes about her experiences, one of which he shared with former Deputy District Attorney John Miner.

Miner proclaimed on the "Marilyn Files Live" television show that he had heard one of the tapes. After listening to its contents, Miner told authorities that he had changed his opinion about her death from suicide to homicide. He promised Greenson that he would never reveal the contents because of confidentiality considerations.

This turned out to be another tape, which could have a bearing on solving the mystery of her death. Although we don't know what information it contained, we can be sure it was at least damaging enough to change Miner's mind. The tape may still be in the possession of the Greenson family.

At least one investigative writer, Donald Spoto, believes Greenson killed Marilyn, and ambulance driver James Hall has stated the same. My investigation suggests that Dr. Ralph Greenson helped orchestrate this intricate cover-up, but could not have acted alone. He didn't have the political power or clout to implement this master plan. He might have been a bullet, but he didn't shoot the gun.

Incidentally 20th Century Fox Studios later produced and released a movie based on the life of Dr. Ralph Greenson. He was paid a whopping $250,000 for the film, "Captain Newman M.D.", which portrayed him as an American hero.

Eunice Murray

Eunice Murray was hired as Marilyn's housekeeper at Greenson's urging. As it turned out, Murray was a trained psychiatric nurse, who had worked nearly fifteen years for Greenson. She apparently had been put there to observe Marilyn's reactions to his Psychoanalytic treatments. In the days leading up to Marilyn's death, the actress had become increasingly concerned about Mrs. Murray, and had began telling her friends, "There's a spy in my house."

Jeanne Carmine stated that Murray was "sneaky" and always seemed "very suspicious." FBI files also listed Eunice Murray as a card-carrying member of the Communist party along with her brother, Churchill Murray, who was a member of an open group of American Communist.

The night of Marilyn's death, Eunice Murray was accused of changing her story about the timeline of the night's events. According to Jack Clemmons, she first stated that she discovered something was wrong sometime around midnight. Later her story was recanted to state it wasn't until 3:30am that she first noticed. During a 1985 BBC interview session with Journalist, Anthony Summers, he claims Murray reverted back to her original story and broke down in tears saying, "Why do I have to continue lying after all of these years?"

It has always been a mystery to me that she didn't hear the fighting and arguing that was taking place in the house that evening. Nearly every investigator ever involved in this case, including myself, believes Eunice Murray knew more than she ever told. If she had been made to testify under oath I'm sure explosive information would have been revealed about the night of August 4, 1962. However, just as many others involved in this case, Eunice Murray has taken all of those secrets to the grave with her, leaving only speculation about what she saw and heard that evening.

THE COMMUNIST CONNECTION

The subject of Communism may be the single largest reoccurring theme throughout this Marilyn saga. From the time Robert Maheu first contacted her, till the moment she died, there was an undeniable communist presence in Marilyn's life. The question is why?

It is important to understand that the war between Capitalism and Socialism was at its peak during Marilyn's lifetime. These opposing political views not only divided our nation, but also divided the entire world. Marilyn was schooled in the ways of communism. However, it wasn't because she was a communist, but rather to be a weapon in the war.

Marilyn was recruited to spy on Arthur Miller's communist activities, according to her diary. A 34-page FBI report, compiled in 1961, says that Miller was identified by an informant as being "under Communist Party discipline." The informant also told the FBI, "Miller became disillusioned with the party because the party did not stimulate in him the ability and inspiration to do creative writing, as he had expected when he joined the party." Could these comments have come from Marilyn?

Marilyn's diary and CIA documents both reveal she also attended secret meetings discussing assassination plans for Fidel Castro. What was Marilyn doing there?

Marilyn's diary, and additional intelligence documents, also say Marilyn helped bring down Indonesian President,

Achmad Sukarno, whose country was allegedly drifting into communist hands. Why was Marilyn selected for this assignment?

Perhaps strangest of all is this: both of Marilyn's doctors and her housekeeper were known communists. Marilyn Monroe died with these people watching over her. After her death, they concocted the story of suicide and spread the tale to everybody who would listen. To this day, that is why the ruling of 'probable suicide' is still on Marilyn's death certificate.

CHAPTER 16:
The Closing Argument

Let me begin my closing argument by saying my fifty-year experience with the Marilyn Monroe investigation has led me to some reasonable conclusions about why this woman was killed. For the majority of those years, I just wanted to understand how she died and why the conspirators set-up me up.

At first glance, when the evidence is examined, these answers seem simple. Somebody obviously gave Marilyn enough drugs to kill her and I interfered with the cover-up plan. However, under closer examination, a much broader picture begins to emerge.

Marilyn's story represents a time in history when our nation was trying to enter its own modernity. America was still defining its future. Her death, tragic as it was, only served to illustrate a fundamental systemic problem, which has become commonplace in this experiment called American Freedom.

The early 20th Century had laid the foundation for an advanced society ready to reach an unlimited potential and become the greatest country on Earth. However, entrenched in this foundation full of promise was a dark side. This iniquity was an untested concept that without proper monitoring and oversight could lead to an abuse of power like nothing else, and it was called Capitalism.

Coming out of World War II, the American workforce was robust, and skilled laborers were at an all time high. Industrialists such as General Motors, Lockheed, General Electric, DuPont, U.S. Steel any many other manufacturers were making money hand over fist, but many laborers were still being paid meager wages. Thus, enter the Union Movement and the organization of the national labor workforce. During the second-world war, Unions had gained significant strength and were becoming involved in every aspect of American labor.

This growth of unions became the single largest threat to the prosperity of big American businesses. Not only did the unions organize the Laborers, but they also utilized the muscle of organized crime to prevent the strike breaking tactics of the Industrialists. To combat this, corporations turned to politicians who could utilize the power of U.S. Government agencies and win back their advantage.

In 1953, Senator Joe McCarthy picked up the banner and devised a plot to create a public panic about the threat of Communism. McCarthy began targeting every group and organization in opposition to America's Capitalism movement. He mounted what became a witch-hunt for American citizen communists. A branch of the United

States Government, called The House Un-American Activities Committee, began accusing and prosecuting people who disagreed with the system.

Hollywood writers were among the first groups to fall into this category of communist. Many writers and producers saw the dark side of capitalism and were creating films and plays that presented negative portrayals of American life. Hollywood's liberal attitude towards socialism and economic equality in America was a problem for the Industrialists' agenda. Play writer Arthur Miller was the most well known name placed on the communist list.

Federal Bureau of Investigation Director, J. Edgar Hoover, also joined the fight. He called Unions, the Civil Rights Movement, and Liberal Government officials the biggest threat to our country's national security. The war against Communism was now an all out battle, and this scenario is what led to this story's most vulnerable victim, Marilyn Monroe.

Examining Marilyn's early life, it's easy to see why she was susceptible to the world of espionage. Being raised as a foster child and never knowing the security that comes from a loving family, shaped Marilyn's life in numerous ways. Her mother was mentally unstable and had once even stuffed Marilyn in a zipped military duffel bag, trying to abduct her from a foster home.

Although Marilyn's early life was very traumatic, she always dreamed of being a Hollywood star. When Robert

Maheu approached her in the mid 1950's, Marilyn thought her career was slipping away. Her contract had been cancelled, the studios were stonewalling her, and here comes the FBI to save the day. Big promises are made to save her career, if she agrees to "*Do something for America.*"

Marilyn became a pawn in a high stakes game of chess, and from the moment she began playing, it was only a matter of time before she was taken. After providing evidence against Arthur Miller, not only did her position in Hollywood advance, but she also became a valuable asset for the U.S. intelligence community. Marilyn was the home court advantage and she knew exactly how to play the role. So when John Kennedy brought her in to those secret meetings with the Central Intelligence Agency and Mafia gangsters, you can believe that all eyes were on her.

In fact, this worked so well that Big Jim O'Connell and the CIA wanted to use her for more sophisticated operations. The war against Communism and Socialist ideas was already extending far beyond our American borders. Capitalism was being implemented around the world, and any country failing to comply with the wealthiest powers were deemed communists, a label which stigmatized them as the bad guys, and even more importantly, as anti-America.

This allowed for vast resources of money being spent to undermine and overthrow foreign governments who wouldn't play ball. Fidel Castro in Cuba and Achmad

Sukarno in Indonesia are two prime examples of what our intelligence community was doing around the world. But what makes all of this so significant is that agencies were recruiting vulnerable American citizens to do their clandestine bidding.

For nearly seven years, this woman was trapped in a world built to devour even the strongest people. The players in this game were powerful and the prizes for winning were beyond comprehension. Yes, they were more than willing to give Marilyn the fame and fortune she desired, but it came with a price, and Marilyn didn't understand the fine print.

Sometime in the midst of Marilyn's real life drama, she began documenting her experiences in a diary. Although we can't be certain exactly when she began writing, my best estimate put its origins sometime around 1960.

The big question we must ask is why Marilyn felt the need to write about events, which obviously involved matters of national security. Certainly she was aware there would be consequences if these details were ever made public. In fact, much of what she wrote was cryptic and took many years of research and fortunate coincidence to decipher.

Marilyn wrote names like Iron Bob and Big Jim, which remained mysteries for decades. Only the research of numerous journalists and the advent of today's information superhighway have allowed me to uncover enough information to discover their true identities. The truth of the matter is, for many years, I believed Bob Slatzer was actually Iron Bob. For the first few years of our relationship, I never mentioned seeing that name in her diary and remained slightly leery of his true intentions concerning me. The possibility always existed that he was part of this grand cover up, but thankfully that never turned out to be the case.

Bob was one of only three other people who have acknowledged reading entries from the same diary that arrived at the Coroner's Office on August 5, 1962. He once told me that Marilyn was just trying to keep track of things, but I believe she was much smarter than most people gave her credit. Marilyn knew she was in way too deep, and she wasn't going down without a fight. Marilyn wrote this journal, and then made sure key friends read parts of diary so they could validate its existence. Once that stage was set, she pulled the biggest trick of all by making sure the book was discovered after she was gone.

After examining the evidence and giving this much consideration, I believe Marilyn played a shell game with her diary. During my years of investigation, there have been multiple sightings of additional diaries allegedly written by Marilyn, none containing the same information I read. Bobby Kennedy and the secret service searched Marilyn's house for it, yet this one was left behind. There is a distinct probability that Marilyn wrote in several diaries, with only one arriving to the Coroner's office.

The controversy surrounding Marilyn Monroe's death was never supposed to happen. Everything had already been put in place to guarantee her death to be quickly written off as suicide. Both of Marilyn's doctors and her housekeeper were persuaded to make false statements to police investigators. These statements were then used to verify her cause of death. With that in hand, detectives at the crime scene were told to release her body to the mortuary. No test would be done, no capsules would be found lodged in her throat, and no toxicology result would show the absence of poison in her stomach. Her body organs would never have had to disappear. Marilyn would have been dead, and there was nothing anyone could have said.

However, as I've said before, something funny happened along the way. A young Deputy Coroner, working the weekend shift that Sunday morning, decided to order Marilyn's body brought to the Coroner's Office. This unexpected event set off of a mad scramble to cover-up evidence at the highest levels of county, city, and federal government.

What has become apparent is that officials at the Los Angeles Police Department, District Attorneys Office and the County Coroner were involved, with all three agencies forced to conceal evidence. As for the public servants working for these agencies that witnessed the cover-ups and spoke out, all were thrown to the sharks and discredited in every imaginable way.

Upon looking at this situation even deeper, the realization sets in that none of these agencies ever had a choice of how to handle these circumstances. Who were they going to prosecute and what witnesses were they going to call? Whose notes were they going to subpoena and what would they expect U.S. Intelligence agents to say? All roads to prosecution were dead ends and the people involved were powerful beyond belief.

I was the first to have the nerve, as one Los Angeles Times reporter said, to reveal what Marilyn had discussed in her conversations with the Central Intelligence Agency and Federal Bureau of Investigations. Most people have never wanted to believe the complicated circumstances surrounding Marilyn's story, including those who officially investigated her case.

My memoir, which documents a 50-year experience with Marilyn's case, has formed the basis for these final conclusions I am presenting.I've told my story too many times to count since 1962, but never in this much detail. My answers concerning the mishandling of information at the Coroner's Office have always been consistent. No County official or employee has ever denied what I've said about missing documents or evidence from Coroner's Case #81128.

This takes us to the days leading up to Marilyn's death. Marilyn was preparing to hold a press conference, which would reveal all of her secrets. During my official investigation, I discovered a typewritten press release in her personal property. Although it contained no date or time and appeared incomplete, its intentions were perfectly clear.

The document stated:

Press Release

Questions and Answers about Marilyn's Diary of Secrets

Event: Marilyn Monroe Press Conference
Place: Los Angeles Press Club
Subject: Marilyn Monroe Reveal's It All
Date:
Time:

For Immediate Release

Marilyn was about to reveal it all. Just think about that. Everything she knew about the Kennedys, everything she had done for the Central Intelligence Agency, the Federal Bureau of Investigation, and everything she had heard about Sam Giancana's Mafia Organization. Marilyn was really about to, as she put it, "Blow the lid off the whole damn thing."

In her diary, Marilyn had written that Peter Lawford was begging her to cancel this press conference, and since then I have discovered that he was not the only one.

Marilyn had told many of her closest friends that she was tired of being used by John and Robert Kennedy. She told Bob Slatzer that she had been promised many things and stood by helplessly as those promises turned into betrayal. Bob said that on the Friday before she died, Marilyn had called him saying that she was trying to get in touch with Bobby Kennedy. He wasn't taking her calls, and she told Bob that if she didn't hear from him by Monday, she was going to hold the press conference.

Marilyn's best friend, Jeanne Carmine, was also aware of the press conference. She said Marilyn was holding the press conference because she was angry at the way Bobby had cut off their relationship. Carmine speculated that if Bobby would have explained his situation better to Marilyn, that things might have gone smoother. However, Marilyn had a bad taste in her mouth and felt scorned. Carmine said she is certain that Marilyn would have told the press everything, and Bobby Kennedy knew she would too.

Both Jeanne Carmine and Bob Slatzer saw real danger for Marilyn ahead and warned her about it. None of this mattered to her, and ultimately she may have made the biggest mistake of her life. One week before she died, Marilyn decided to attend one of Frank Sinatra's parties in Lake Tahoe. There, in a drunken state of mind, she began telling partygoers about the press conference she was planning. Those in attendance included Sam Giancana and

Jimmy Hoffa, who both initiated their own wiretap on Marilyn's house. The following Saturday night, they would record the infamous fight between Marilyn and Bobby. The next day she was found dead.

In 1982, the last official public inquiry into Marilyn Monroe's death was held. Los Angeles County Assistant District Attorney Ronald Carroll headed the investigation. In his final report, Carroll stated, "Our investigators reviewed the 20-year-old results of Dr. Theodore Curphey's Coroner's investigation. They were proclaimed to be accurate and we stand behind the Suicide Investigation Team's findings." Carroll went on to say, "Marilyn's doctors declared in their professional opinion that she was not in a state of mind to write anything constructive. He found no evidence that Marilyn's book was ever in the Coroner's Office." This was despite multiple accounts to the contrary.

Often I wondered why Carroll, who had worked hard to get where he was, would so blatantly ignore obvious facts staring him in the face. But again, what choice did he have? Ron Carroll was a civil service worker just as Jack Clemmons, John Miner, and myself. The only difference was that he knew the rules: play ball or suffer the consequences.

Carroll's boss, Los Angeles County District Attorney John Van De Kamp, would imply that we had made this all up. Why would he think we had nothing better to do than lie to a County Official, while seeking to testify under oath to the grand jury? As it turns out, there was never a serious attempt to discover the truth during this investigation. The District Attorney had based all its conclusions on witnesses who were either lying or involved in this cover-up.

Dr. Ralph Greenson, whose professional opinion was the basis of the report, had died in 1978 before the inquiry began. By then however, Greenson had already recanted his belief that Marilyn was suicidal, according to Deputy District Attorney John Miner. Carroll disregarded this vital piece of information and decided not to use Miner's statements in his final report.

Miner was not the only witness whose testimony was disregarded. Jeanne Carmine also told investigators about reading Marilyn's diary. She also told them about Marilyn's relationship with Bobby Kennedy and her threats about going public with matters of national security.

Jack Clemmons, the first police officer on the scene, testified that witnesses had changed their stories about the night's events. District Attorney investigators ignored him, ultimately omitting any information that conflicted with the original Coroner's findings.

In all, three public officials, representing the Coroner's Office, District Attorney's Office, and Police Department testified during this inquiry about Marilyn's case. However, Van De Kamp and his investigation team cast them all aside.

Recent Government disclosures have now established Marilyn's involvement with the intelligence community, and it is my belief this had something to do with her death.

Our federal government knows the answer to this web of deceit. Only the Freedom of Information Act appeal-process shows any hope of answering the call of the people. In that regard, writing this book has been a powerful experience. My research proves that more revealing information exists. A debate is under way in the CIA's Agency Release Panel, concerning whether to release existing documents on Marilyn Monroe. It seems strange for the CIA to debate with itself over releasing these documents, because since the beginning the Agency has claimed to have no documents regarding Marilyn Monroe. However, as we know, information to the contrary has continued to surface over the years, and when the CIA's hand has been forced new documents always pop up.

It seems that modern day bureaucrats are determining what information should be released to the American Public. Given what is now known about their complicity in Marilyn's death, and in the deaths of the other people who are a part of this story, it must be some incriminating information. I remember reading what J. Edgar Hoover, head of the FBI, said to a friend when told of the Robert Kennedy assassination; "I know that the CIA and their hit man Robert Maheu did it and there is nothing I can do about it."

I once heard a professor from the University of California say,

"Its Not Truth Until Its Written Down."

If you still don't understand why this story has lasted for 50 years, after you've read this account of Marilyn Monroe's death, then I haven't done a good job explaining it. This story has been about a massive cover-up, where powerful government officials conspire to hide the truth from the American Public. It is a bold example of how bureaucrats wield their power without any regard for American citizens, and lack the desire to tell the truth.

I've given plenty thought to what national security issues could explain why one of these agencies has never come forward with the details. I believe the answer is simple; it involves the assassination of one of our Presidents and a U.S. Senator. That alone may keep this case a mystery forever.

In closing let me add a little tidbit. My co-author and researcher has been nudging me in the side since the start, wanting to know about my opinion about this case. He told me, "No sane person would compile this kind of data without any conclusion as to who killed Marilyn Monroe, or if she really committed suicide. You are the only one still alive, who was there when the investigation began. Step out on a limb. Tell us who did it."

My response to him was that I was only looking for the cause of death. I was a Coroner's investigator, not a policeman. My thoughts were that once we found out how she died, it would be easy to conclude whom, if anybody, carried out this plot to silence Marilyn. After 50 years, the list of suspects is larger than ever. The complex cover up of evidence that could solve this case is still ongoing.

I close with a word to Marilyn.

On August 6th, 1962 when I walked into the autopsy room and saw you lying on that gurney, the only thought that went through my mind was that your lifestyle had certainly aged you. Your body looked tired and beaten down, but now I understand what you had been through. I hope this book reveals what you wanted to the American Public. I tried to do it some justice. In my eyes, you will always twinkle.

Samir

Made in the USA
Lexington, KY
20 February 2013